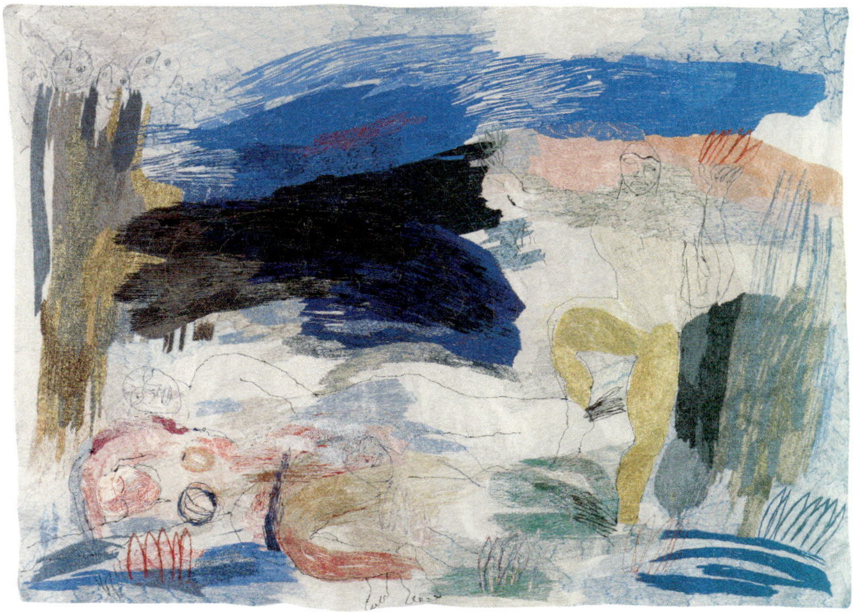

Lotos-Eaters and Hermes – in memory of Evie

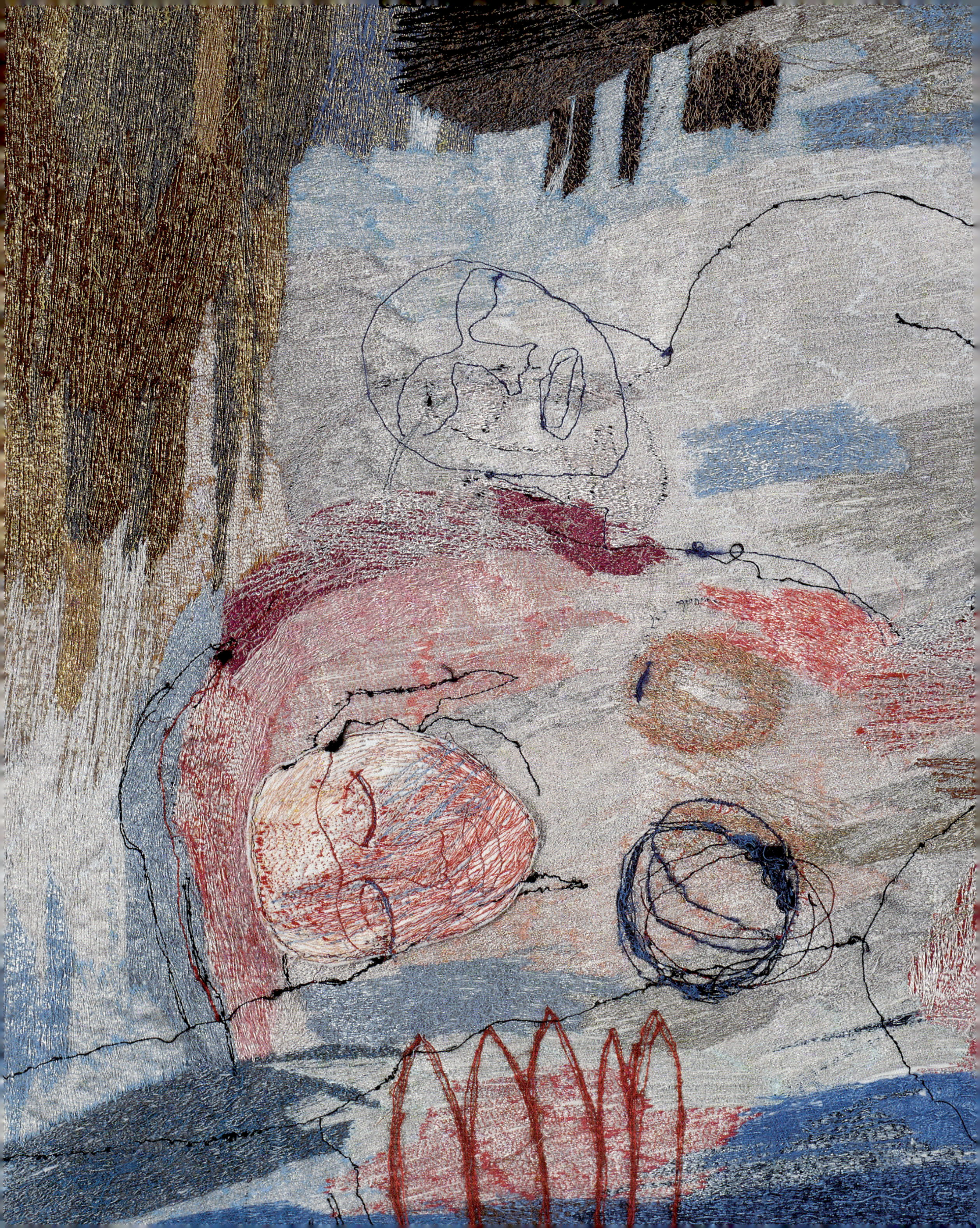

Alice Kettle

mythscapes

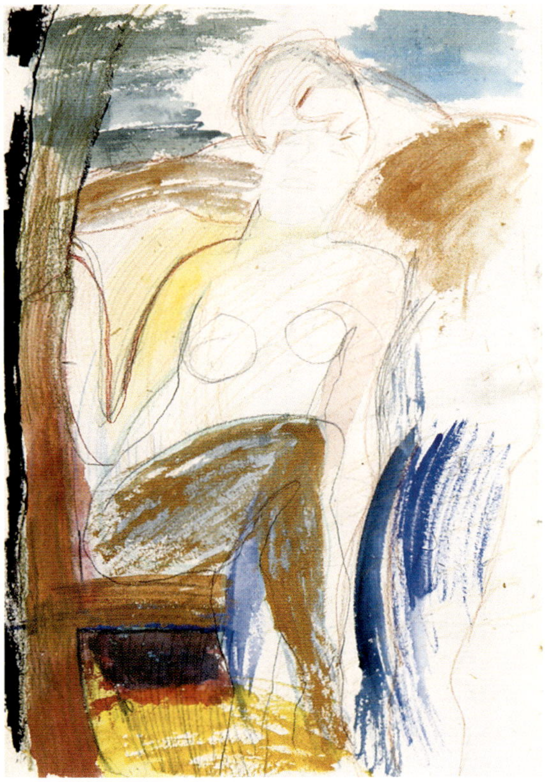

Penelope's Bed I sketch

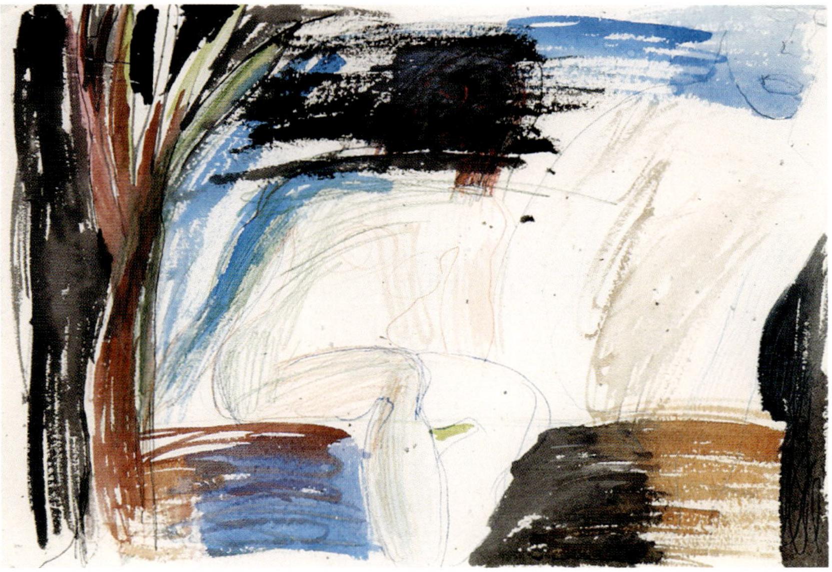

Penelope's Bed II sketch

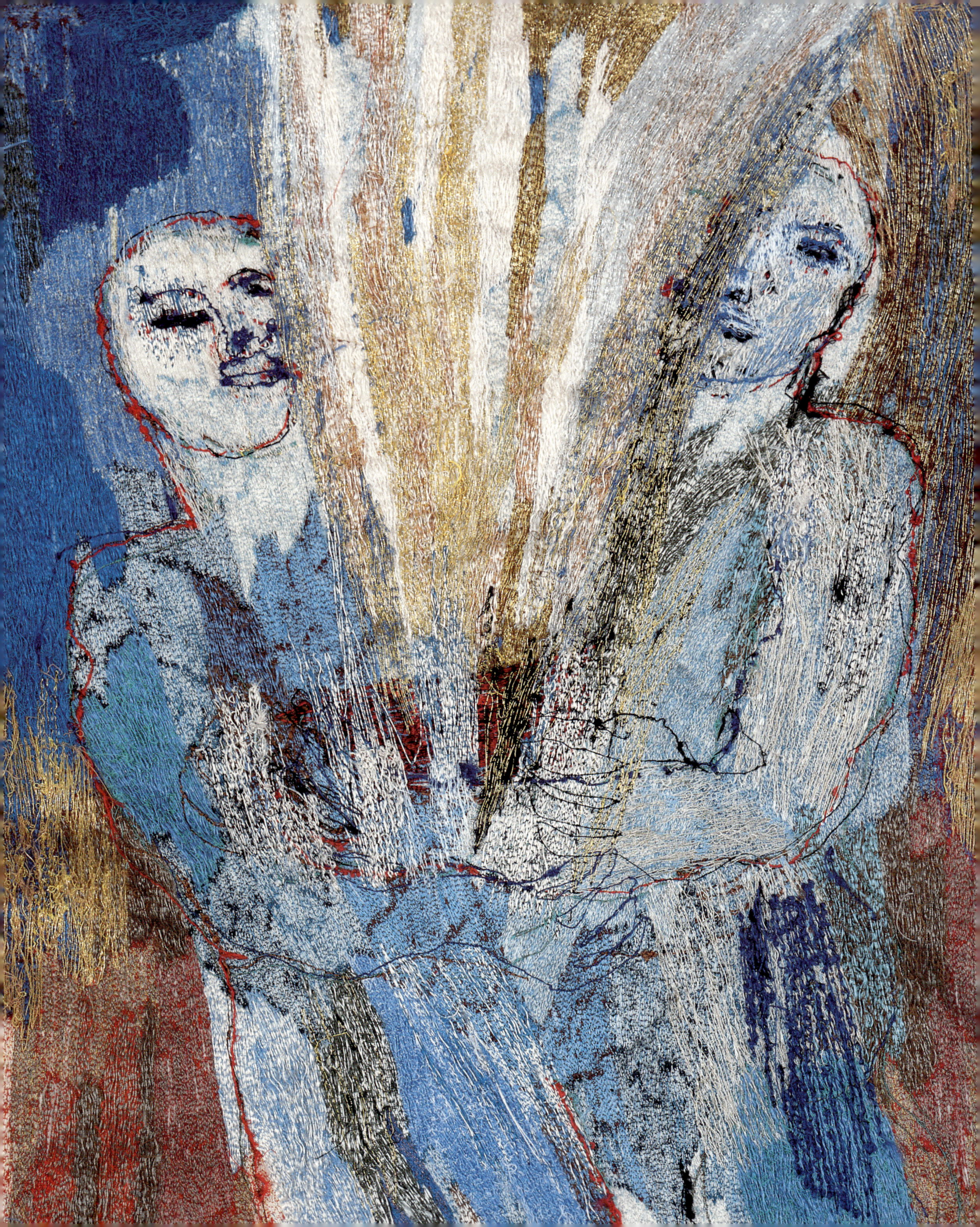

Contents

Bag of Winds

Introduction:

Journey to Mythscapes

In December 2000, we embarked on a mission to acquire a piece of work by Alice Kettle for the collections at Bankfield. Having actively purchased and commissioned a series of works by contemporary artists over a period of eleven years, we were conscious that the absence of any example of Alice's work represented a significant omission within the existing collection of textiles.

We achieved our initial goal, purchasing *Trees 2* with support from the V&A Purchase Grant Fund. At the same time, we set ourselves another goal: inviting Alice to exhibit a body of work at Bankfield at some future date. *Mythscapes* is the result of that invitation and the culmination of over two years of planning and making.

From the early days of the project, Alice has always viewed it as an opportunity to stretch herself as an artist and maker and, in so doing, to define her practice for the next decade. This she has done, through the creation of a major body of new work exploring some of the universal themes raised in Homer's *Odyssey*.

That Alice, aware of the weight of expectation that exists, has retained this creative focus and continued to develop ideas, whilst also being involved in the physically demanding production of the work over such a length of time and amidst all

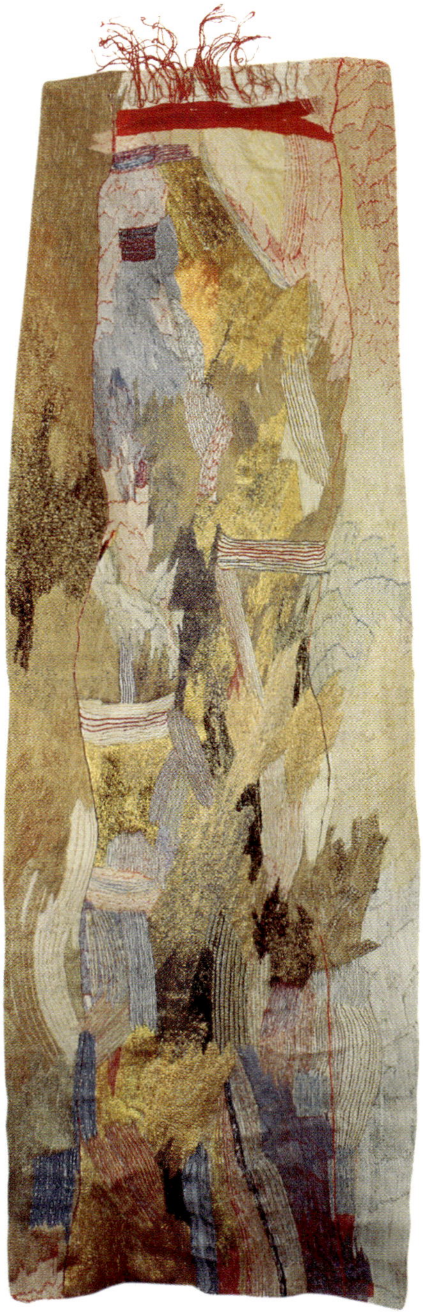

Trees 2

the commitments and diversions of daily life, is a testament to her as both an artist and an individual. *Mythscapes* is a singular achievement by an exceptional artist.

Mythscapes not only defines Alice's practice as an artist, however. In so many ways, it also defines and illustrates Bankfield's practice as an institution.

Since the appointment of Henry Ling Roth as its first Curator in 1900, Bankfield has been actively involved in the field of textiles, gaining worldwide recognition for its historic, cross-cultural and contemporary collections. Alongside the collection, there has been a longstanding commitment to encouraging a greater awareness and understanding of textiles as an accessible medium that crosses disciplines and acts as a bridge between fine and applied art forms.

Bankfield is rooted in an area that produced textiles for a worldwide market for over four hundred years. This brought considerable wealth and fame to the area, reflected today in the architecture of the towns and villages of Calderdale. It also impacted on the lives of its people, many of whom were employed in the manufacture of textiles or textile machinery. Today, although the mass production of textiles is no more, the crafts and creative industries remain a significant part of the life of the area.

Since 1989, thanks to support from Calderdale MBC, The Arts Council and Yorkshire and Humberside Area Museums Council, Calderdale Museums and Arts has worked to develop Bankfield as an institutional advocate for textiles. Through the creation of permanent galleries, the commissioning of new work by contemporary makers and a programme of temporary exhibitions and related workshops and education activities, the intention has been to encourage access to, and involvement in, textiles. The aim above all is to engage with people, to build relationships with users and to create opportunities for mutual development and growth.

Mythscapes embodies this ethos. From an initial proposal between Alice as an individual artist and Bankfield as a venue, the project has grown to involve and encompass many different people and organisations. Each has added significantly to the development of the final product. It has been a privilege to be involved in such a venture. It is an honour to be able to present such an exceptional body of contemporary work to both a national and an international audience.

June Hill
Museum Manager, Bankfield
Calderdale Museums and Arts

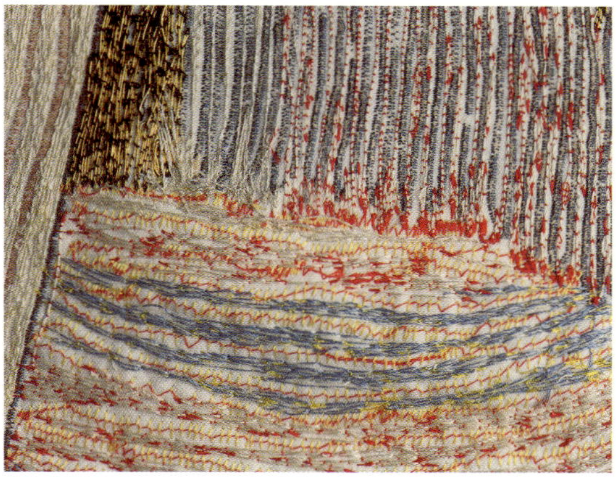

Trees 2 (detail)

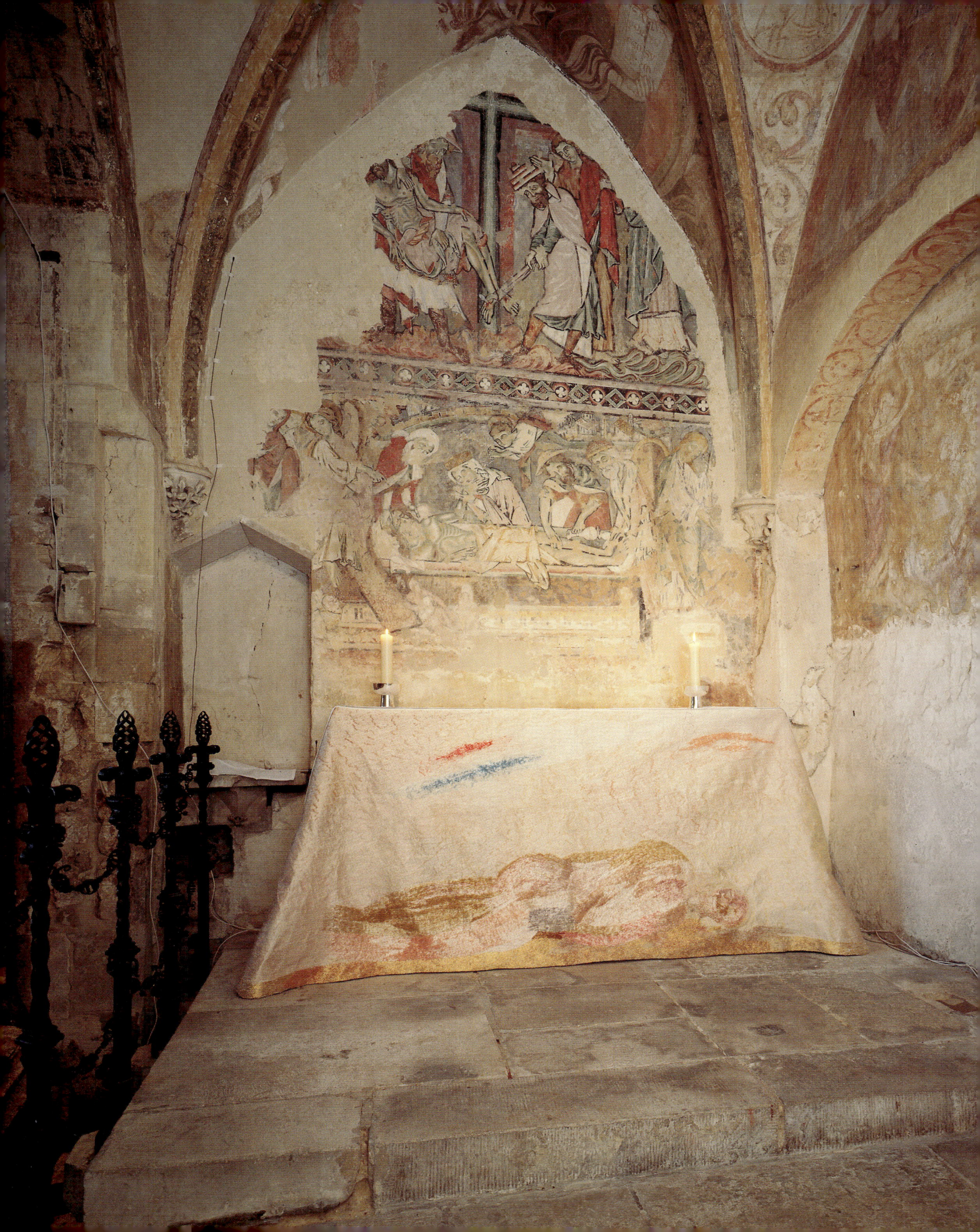

Conversations across time:

Audrey Walker with Alice Kettle

Firstly, the time and the place – 1985, and my small office in Goldsmiths' College where we held interviews for student places on the Postgraduate Diploma Course in Textiles. Alice Kettle (recently graduated from the Fine Art Course at Reading University) came in with her portfolio of work. Even now, eighteen years later, I recall the immediate excitement I felt as the portfolio was opened up and one after another a series of small paintings was revealed. The scale was modest but the impact of the colour was huge – here was someone who clearly knew how to handle colour. A closer look showed that these paintings were peopled with small figures and that this engagement with the human presence was the essential core of the work. Our conversation continued about these people, their stories, their apparent containment and Alice's meditations on them. Finally one small, rather rough embroidery came to light – collaged, machined and primitive though it was, it showed that Alice had an instinctive ability to handle fabric and thread in an expressive way. It seemed that Alice's mother had imbued in her, from childhood, a love of these materials so that they became a perfectly natural resource to give form to imaginative ideas.

Alice is a slightly built, softly spoken and seemingly fragile young woman and during this first conversation I imagined that she would probably continue to work on an intimate scale, perhaps even by means of hand embroidery. Little did I realise how profoundly Alice's work was to be altered and indeed liberated by one mundane factor – a room full of industrial sewing machines! What soon became

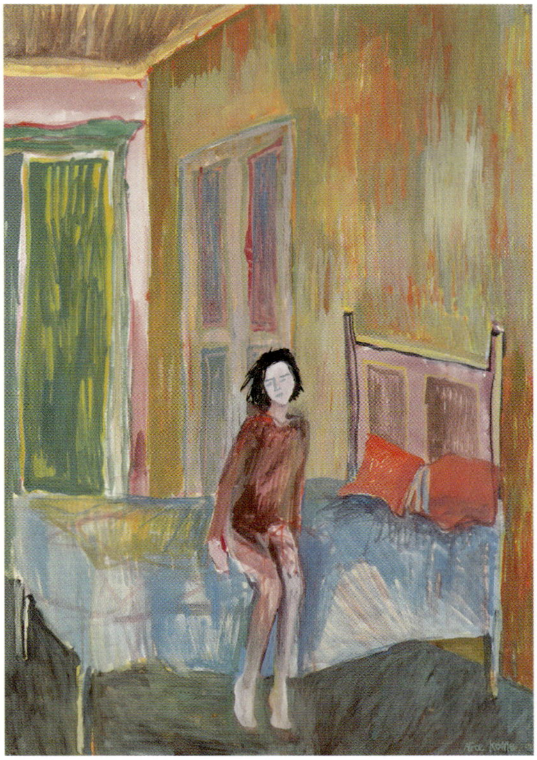

Winchester Cathedral, Sepulchre Chapel Altar Cloth
Girl in her room 1983

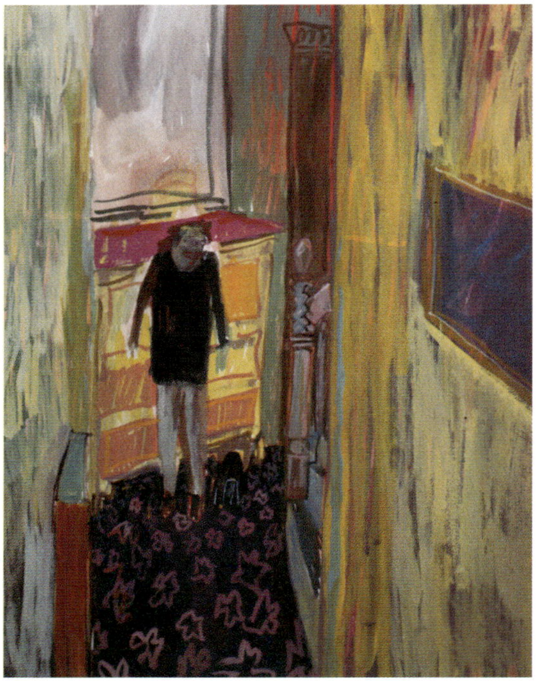

Painting 1982

apparent on the year's course was Alice's determination to make these machines work for her in unprecedented ways. Physical stamina was needed (as in a sculptor) to allow her to handle many yards of fabric, greatly increasing the scale of her work and challenging both herself and pre-conceptions of what embroidery might be as she developed her subject matter. Against the prevailing trends towards abstraction Alice's work was always figurative and she sought ways to make the figures more animated, to become more expressive of gesture or mood. Her machined textiles expanded to stretch down the wall and spill out on to the floor – the nature of textiles was allowing her freedom from the rectilinear format. Her 'end of year' show made an enormous impression on all who saw it.

In the next eighteen years circumstances meant that Alice and I only met occasionally and the 'conversations across time' were between Alice and her subject matter. I witnessed her growing eloquence in the late 1980s when I saw her Dancers, Angels, Harlequin, Pulchinella and Nymphs jump for joy and through the 'nineties saw her accomplish monumental pieces for specific sites. We share a love of Greece and what that implies. There is exposure to the clear light, to intense blues, white, gold, pink and terracotta and to a land so burnt up in the heat that some colours are bleached out to a silvery grey. These colours and that mysterious quality 'light' can all be found in Alice's work, achieved by means of layer upon layer of the separate lines of thread. Beyond these purely physical attributes of the Greek landscape Alice has responded to the ancient myths of Greece and her Heroes and Caryatids have claimed attention alongside Eve and the Madonna. In Alice's hands these iconic figures are usually monumental and heroic but they also, and importantly, contain feelings of vulnerability and tenderness – qualities which can always be discerned in her work.

Perhaps one of the most telling expressions of this vulnerability and the need for tenderness and pity is in the Altar frontal which Alice made in 1994 for the Holy Sepulchre Chapel in Winchester Cathedral. It is far removed from the formulaic designs which are usual in much contemporary ecclesiastical work. The altar itself is surrounded by fragments of medieval

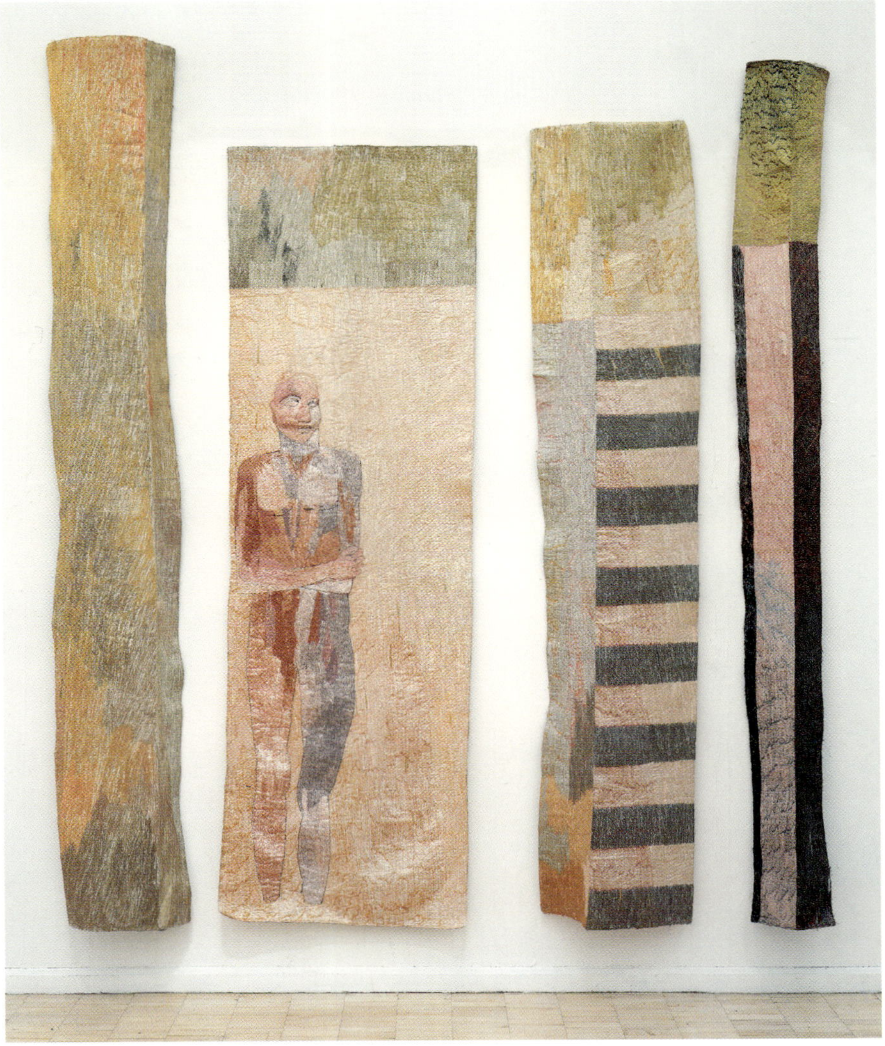

Creation

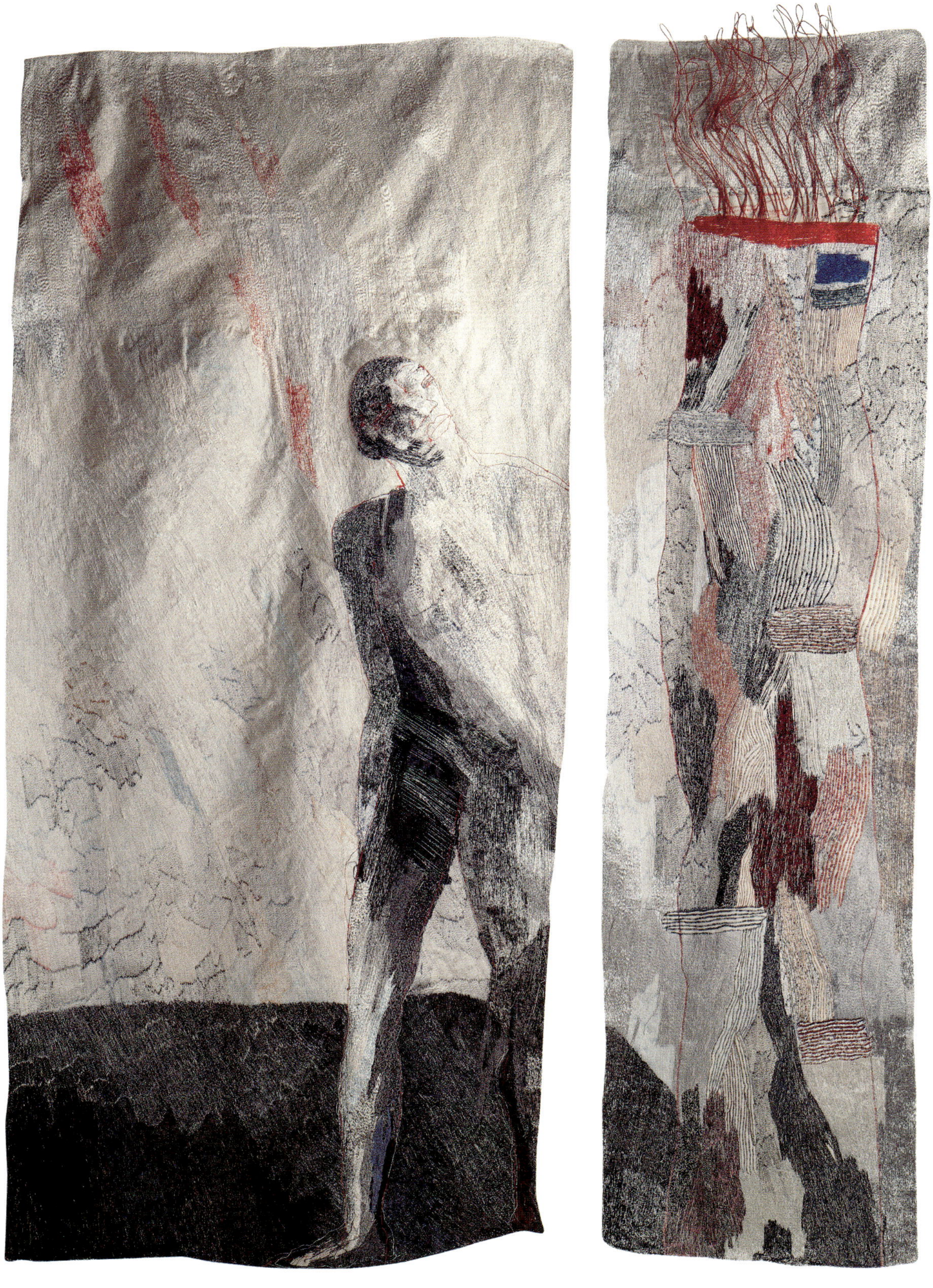

Man and Tree

From dialogue to monologue:

Contextualising the work of Alice Kettle

It is easy to get carried away with the concept of textiles as analogies for human experience, since every language abounds with phrases such as 'the rich tapestry of life', 'following the thread of a conversation', 'spinning a yarn' and many more. But in the work of Alice Kettle there is every reason to examine these plays on words, not least because her focus has consistently pivoted around an exploration of the human condition. While others may claim to have done the same, none have taken up this theme in such an open, accessible way.

When, in 1986, her Goldsmiths' postgraduate show caused such a stir, it did so for a triumvirate of reasons: her painterly use of machine stitching, the large scale of her panels, and their figurative content. Today the last named feature is more difficult to appreciate; the rendering of people in textiles is no longer the rarity it was then. But at the time, the legacy of monumental fibre works of the 1960s and 1970s had established abstract materiality (form, technique, colour and texture) as the only legitimate content for those embarking on a 'serious' textile discourse. The exceptions were few. Among these were *Backs* – the groundbreaking 1976–82 studies of human form made of jute, burlap and resin by the Polish textile artist, Magdalena Abakanowicz. Exhibited in large groups, the impact of Abakanowicz's hunched, headless figures derived from their anonymity, a feature that launched a raft of later visual essays on the 'disembodied'. In the United States, Mary Bero's influential stitched, painted and stuffed exploration of faces and single features (an eye, a mouth) began in the early 1980s; yet these were – and still are – positioned within the specific genre of urban primitivism or indigenous tribalism. They are also very small, seldom exceeding 25cm in any direction. It was Alice Kettle who more than anyone else broke the mould. Her work is monumental but not political. In addition, each piece may begin as an act of autobiography but it ends in universality. Increasingly, even indications of gender began to fade. By 1991, when *Creation* was completed, the principal figure was already reduced to something recognisably human but neither overtly male or female, eastern or western.

Alluding to 'the rich tapestry of life' calls forth the other debate into which Kettle's work was launched. This surrounded tapestry making itself. Already emergent was the Edinburgh School (propelled by weavers at the Dovecot Studios and their close involvement with the tapestry department in the same city's college of art), which challenged the painting-to-tapestry continuum, in which the weavers were to a greater or lesser degree in charge of the

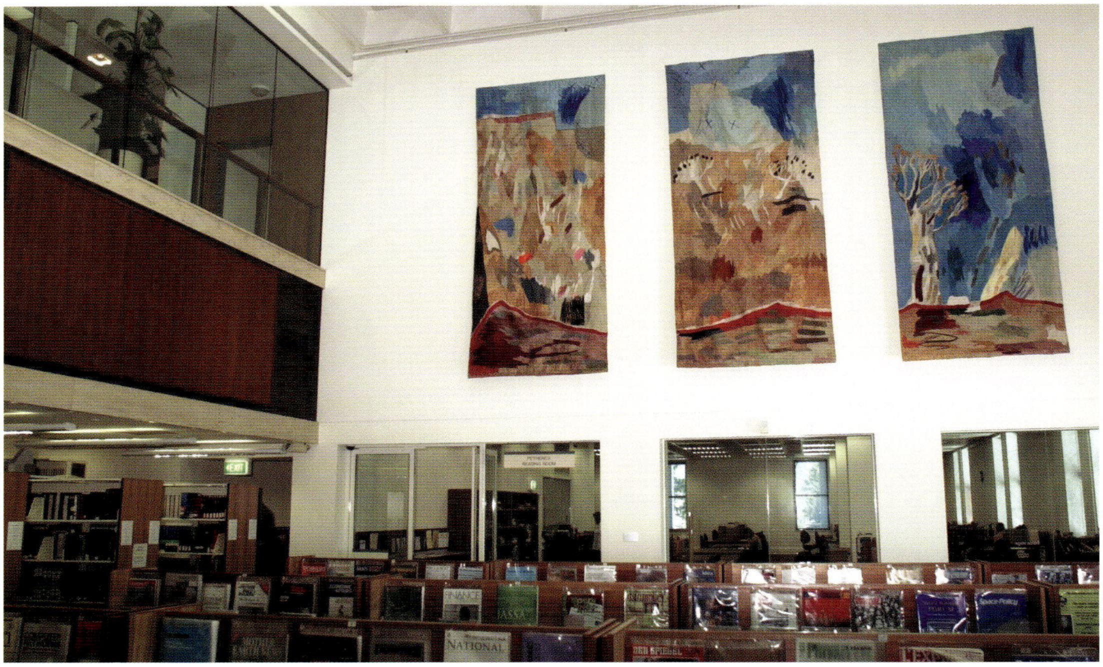

final imagery. Among those weaving their own designs, only a handful of adventurous souls – such as Archie Brennan and Lynne Curran – incorporated the human form. This was perhaps because, however free the interpretation, to do so suggested too closely the long tradition of artists' cartoons slavishly copied in tapestry ateliers. The unveiling of the West Dean Tapestry Studio's Henry Moore figure study tapestries – begun in 1976 but not given wide public exposure until the mid-1980s – only added flames to this particular fire. Within this context Kettle's approach offered a new trajectory. Tapestry-like in their painterly execution as well as in their scale, her figurative panels nevertheless came unburdened with historical precedents. Kettle's technique is thoroughly modern, for while machine embroidery has been explored for artistic ends since the 1930s, hers is the first to exploit its rhythmic, gestural qualities in such an overt manner. The element of risk involved in so often working from the back of the ground cloth makes hers a practice firmly situated in postmodernist thought. Visual evidence of accidents, chaos and revision writhe and wrestle across the surface. Yet Kettle does not seek nor produce the discordant, but rather what she describes as *"harmony, a desire for lyrical*

Australian Landscape series I-IV

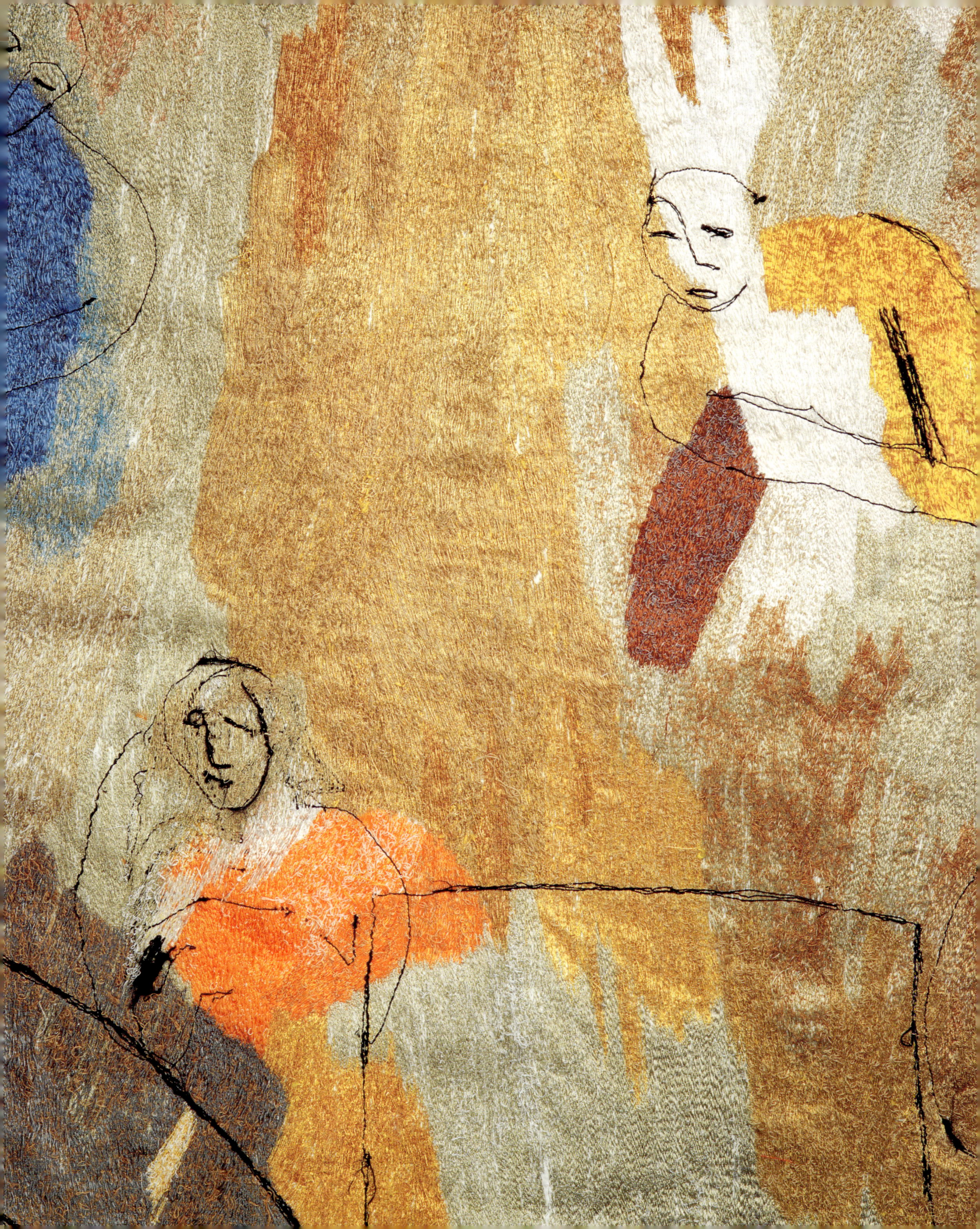

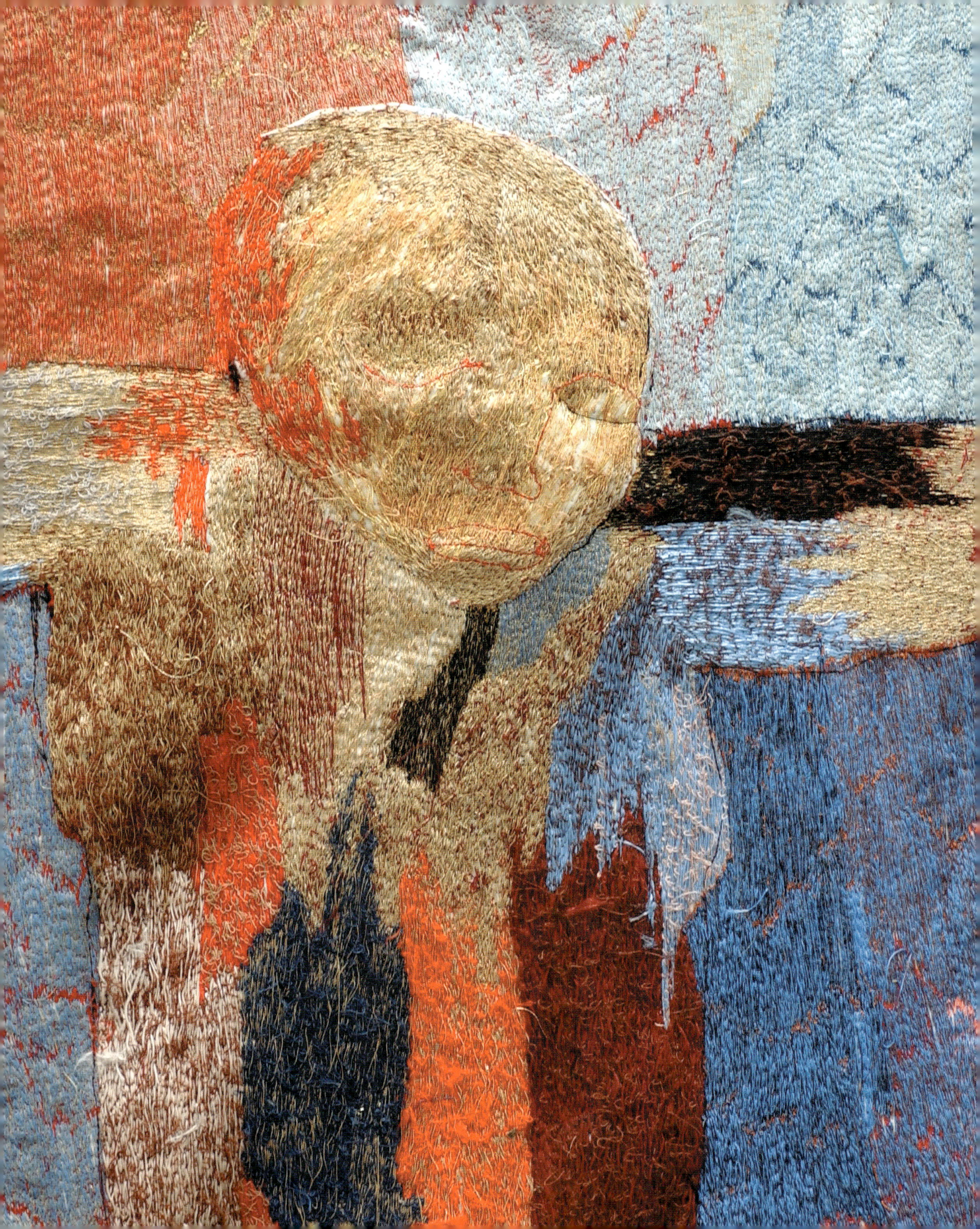

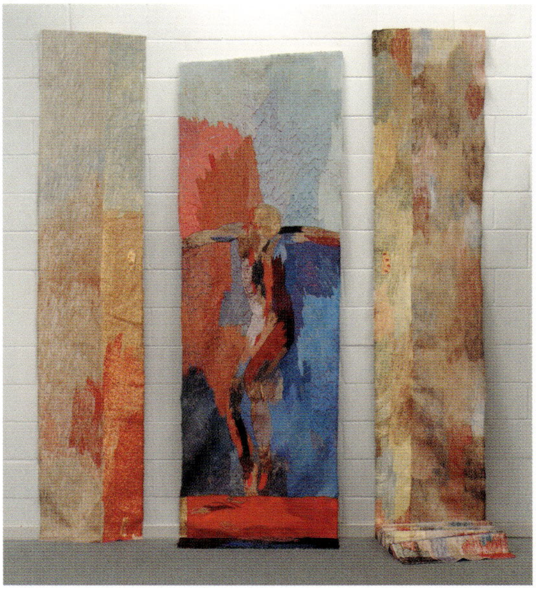

movement…". Despite this, were they musical scores, they would belong with the aleatory or 'chance' school, while the tapestry weavers' challenge – to overcome the technical formality of warp and weft interlocks – produces a stately march.

As to the 'thread of a conversation', Kettle's own words again indicate their relevance. During 1997, while an artist-in-residence at the Australian National University, she was *"captivated by the 'scribbly-gums' with trunks scarred by the channels of burrowing insects."* Her *Man and Tree II* of 1998, developed in response to these, is *"a conversation between colour and line and light, and a dialogue between a person and a tree."* The discourse between landscape and people was further explored in the commission resulting from her residency, *Australian Landscapes I–IV*, which were installed in the National Library of Australia (NLA) in September 2000. The concept of a conversation is also evident in the development of work for *Mythscapes*. Taking *Creation* as a starting point, she has elected to juxtapose its celebration of life, expressed through pure form, to a triptych incorporating the more three-dimensional element of pleating and done in response to the events of September 11th, 2001. She stresses that the latter (*Towers*, 2002) is not political, but simply states that suffering exists. To underscore the dialectic presented in such opposing themes, a third piece (*Rites of Passage*, 2003) has been created to complete the group. Resting on the floor, its carpet-like position – complete with footprints and resonant of the fabled Talmud flying carpet – confirms that her theme is of passages. Here the connecting 'thread' is the journey of every

Towers

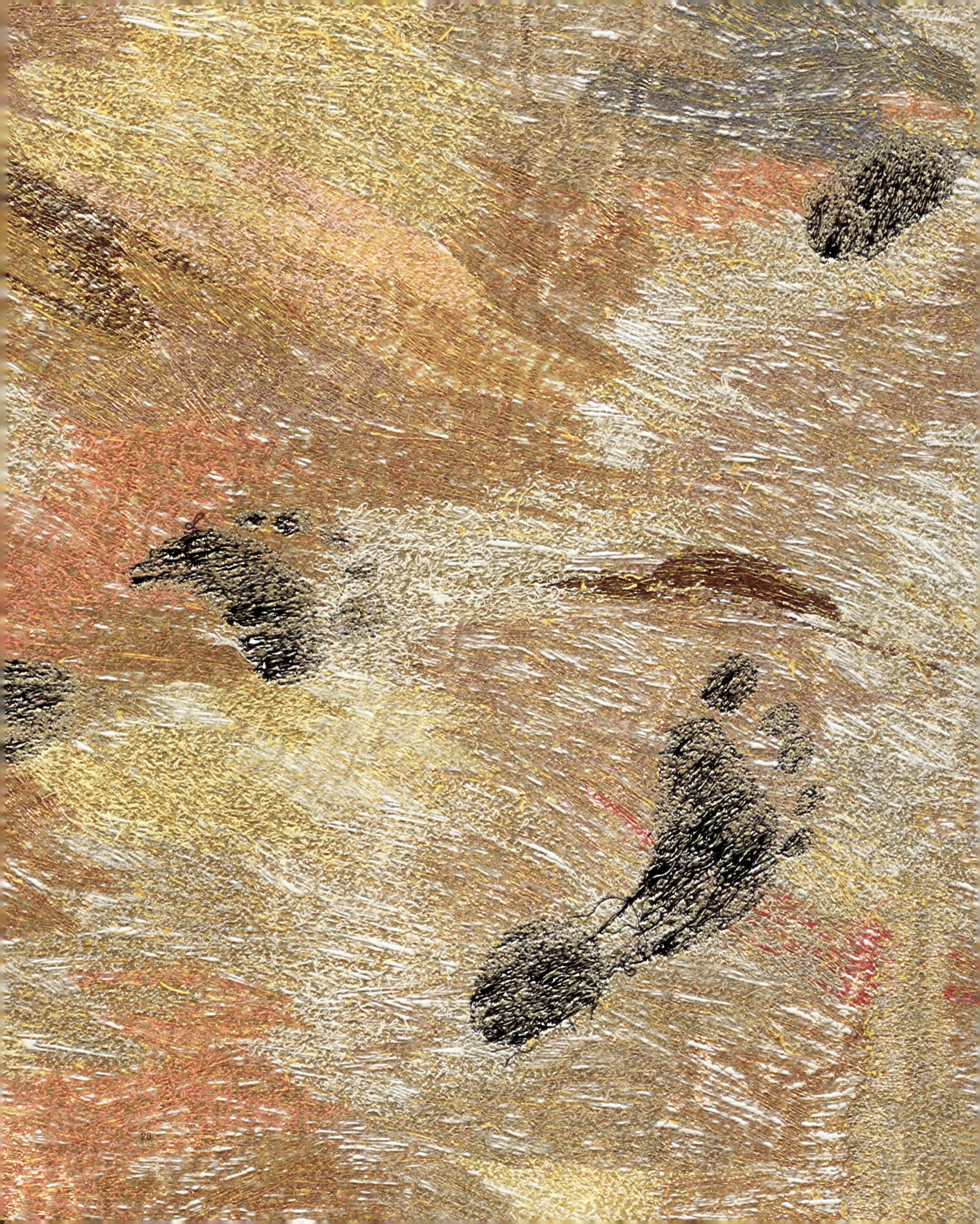

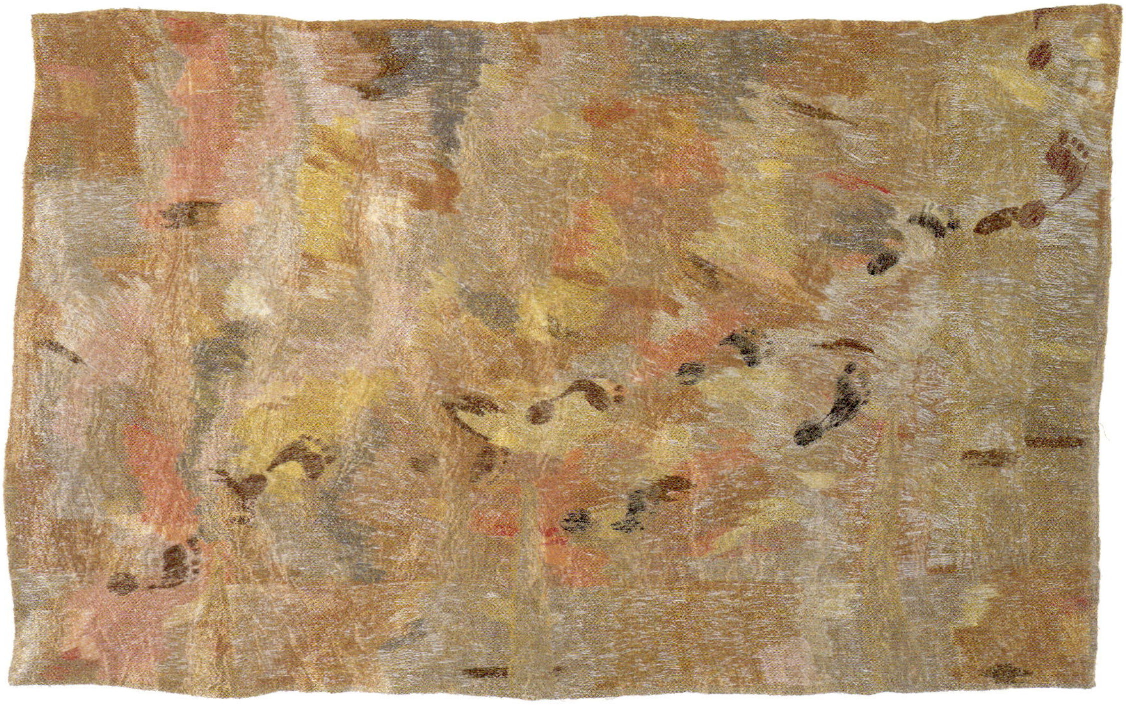

life, expressed literally in threads. These are a constant source of inspiration for Kettle; one might propose an idea, while several together suggest to her relationships. In these ways, she engages in a private colloquy with her materials.

With the conversation between pieces begun, Kettle has recently set herself the most demanding task of her career to date, the *Odyssey* series, also made especially for this exhibition. The massive centrepiece (*Odyssey*, 2003) is the first in which the principal parlay of ideas occurs within a single piece rather than between two or more. Although the shift is subtle, it has powerful resonances. In setting out to depict an epic journey, Kettle has placed herself in the position of narrator. It is her first 'monologue'. Drawing on her love of stories and deep interest in the balance, dignity and strength of classical form, she has 'spun a yarn' essentially about the evolution of ideas and the development of character and resolve. As if to test herself to the limit, she also elected not to use her established format, in which the long and narrow composition most readily facilitates the variation of tempo in the machine stitches, themselves dependent upon manoeuvring the entire panel back and forth under the needle. Instead, *Odyssey* was made in a landscape format and thus technically far more challenging. Even as it was nearing completion she still found that it *"felt dangerous".* Nevertheless, from someone who likes *"doing huge things that tower above you"*, this chancy departure was the logical next step.

Rite of Passage

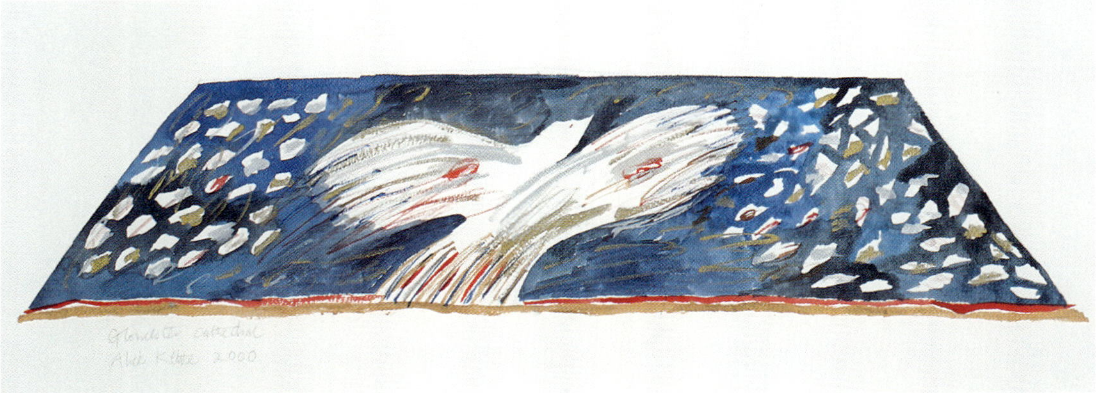

Gloucester Cathedral Altar Cloth: Advent/Lent Frontal

Strolling through Winchester Cathedral with the artist, it also comes as no surprise that, having gone there to give me her own commentary on the Holy Sepulchre Chapel altar frontal, completed in 1994, she elects to exit by way of a tour of the other contemporary pieces commissioned by the Cathedral. She lingers longest in the crypt, inhabited only by Antony Gormley's lone figure (*Sound II, 1989*), contemplating his hands. *"This"*, she says, *"is the most spiritual piece here…"*. It is a remark that brings home the isolation of her working practice as, alone in her garden studio, she sustains her creative vision for the dozen and more months it takes to complete a single project. (For example, the NLA panels, each nearly 4m long, took 18 months to complete.) In addition, it epitomises her lack of pose, a characteristic confirmed by her animated description of the leaving present for the Reverend Canon Keith Walker, who had instigated and sustained the Cathedral's policy of enlightened commissioning. Each previously commissioned artist was given a standard-sized piece of paper on which to produce a drawing; to Kettle's delight, when bound in alphabetical order for the presentation volume, her work closely followed Gormley's. Can this really be the maker of *Glimpses of India*, a six-panel suite made in 1994–5 for the P&O liner, the MV Oriana, and said to be the largest embroideries in existence? Or the person described in the official website of the NLA as a 'world-renowned English artist'?

This is not to suggest that Kettle is ignorant of her audience or the expectations placed upon her as a result of previous successes. Far from it. She has toyed with the idea of changing her working methods. She has considered the demands of satisfying commissions, something that has increasingly occupied her time since 1994. Time, she has concluded, is the critical factor. The laborious nature of her creative practice allows for long periods of free-wheeling imaginative thought – often about

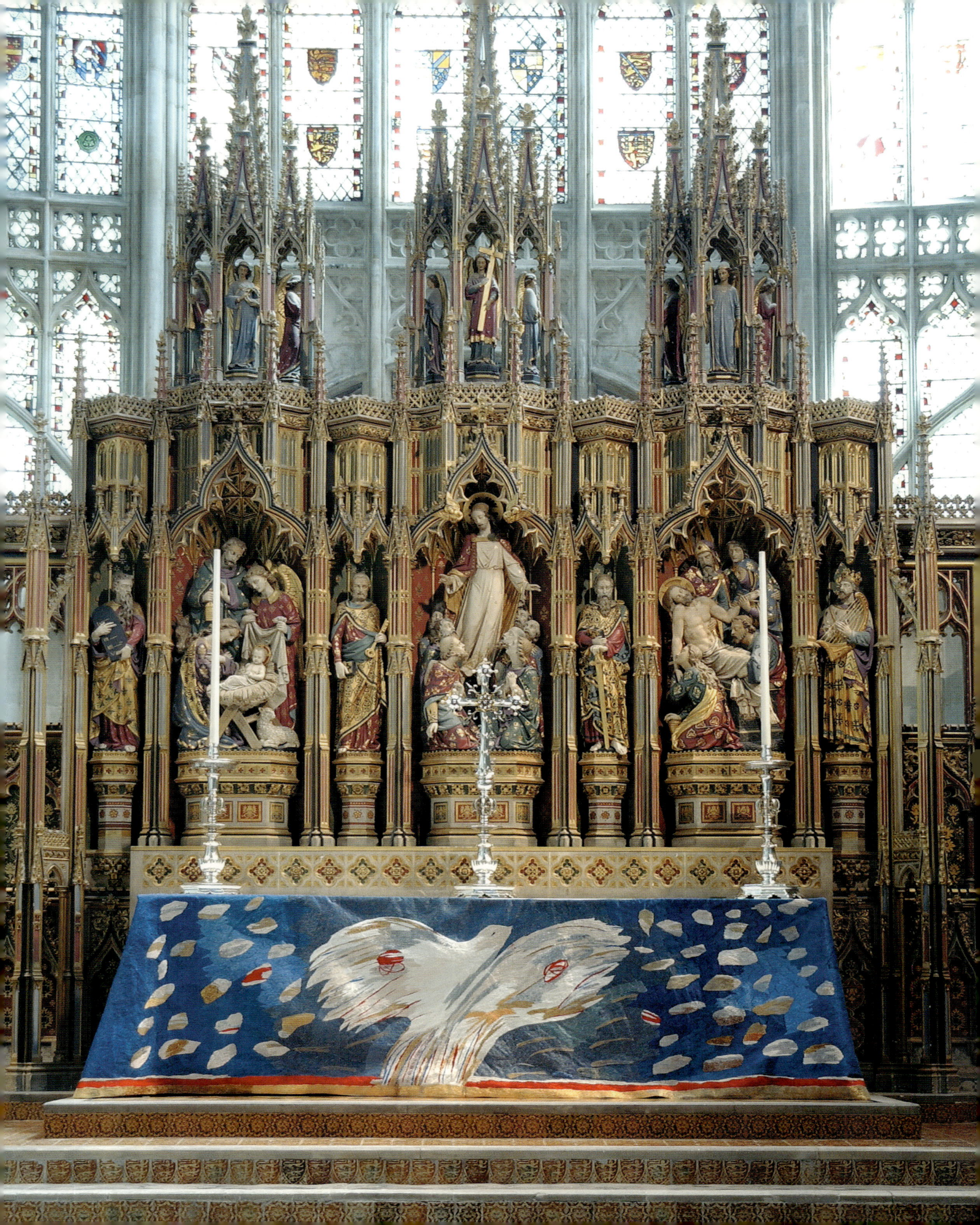

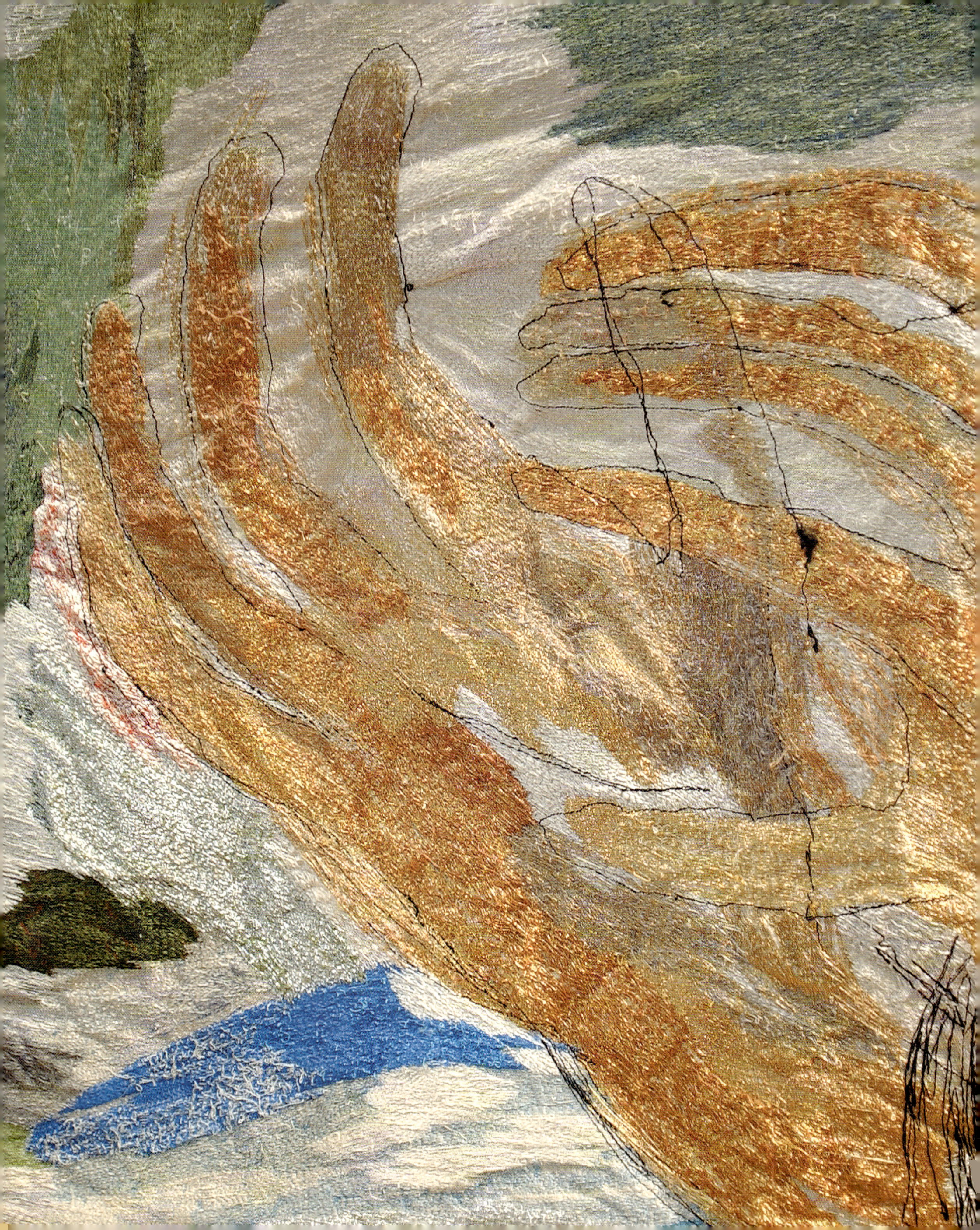

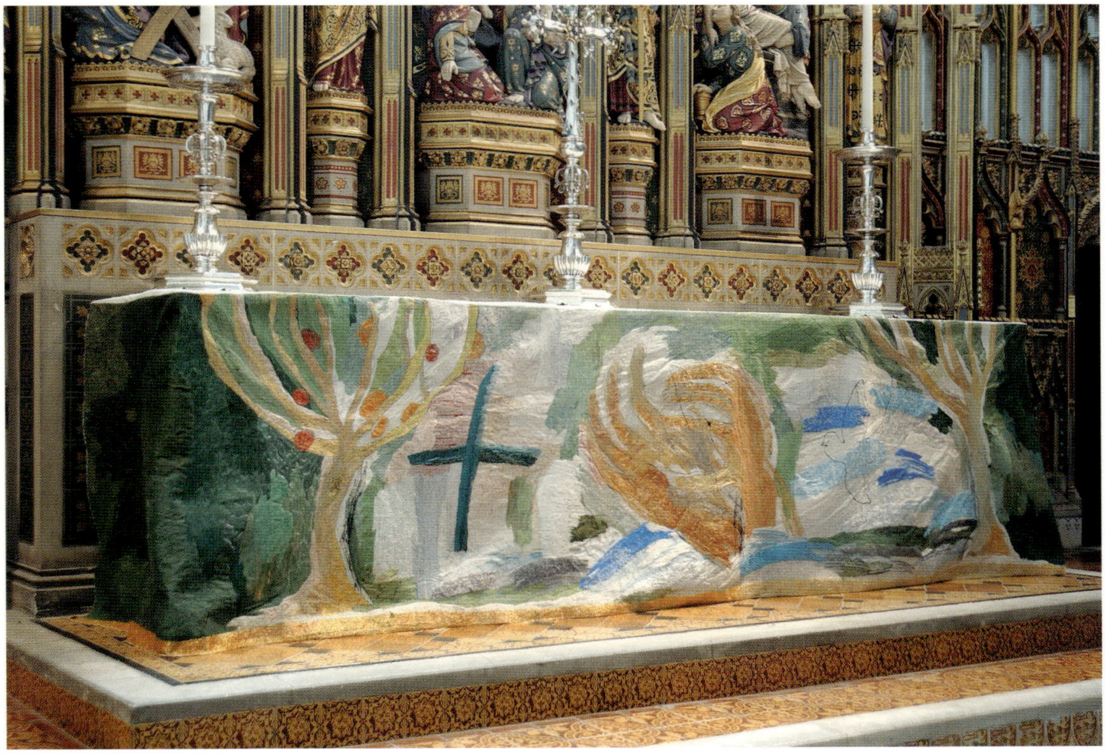

Trinity Frontal

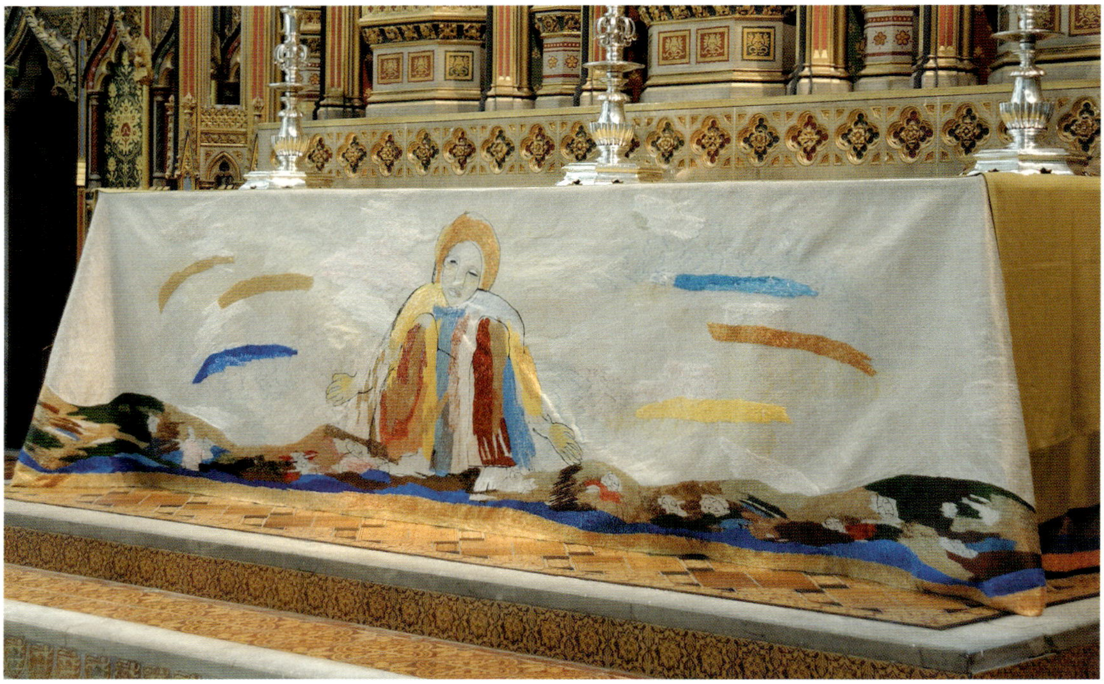

the next piece. The pressure of a time-frame fixed by clients is off-set by the chance to respond to a particular place and space, to exercise her belief that textiles are the ideal bridge between different media and therefore intrinsically architectural. Thus in her three High Altar frontals completed for Gloucester Cathedral in 2001, she recognised that she wanted to bring movement and dynamic force into an often-static scene, while in *Chagall Column* – placed in Chichester Cathedral in the same year – her commission was to compose a three-dimensional work bringing together the themes of windows (including the Chagall at Tudeley), with the concepts celebration and colouration in direct reference to the Cathedral's Chagall window. Nevertheless, things have changed. Her foray into narrative and the landscape format marks the emergence of a mature artist entering what will undoubtedly be a more public phase of her career. Finished are her days of self-examination, so exposed and yet hidden within the *Odyssey* series. The work speaks for itself, freeing Kettle to say with resolved certainty, *"I must do this…".*

Mary Schoeser

Festivals Frontal

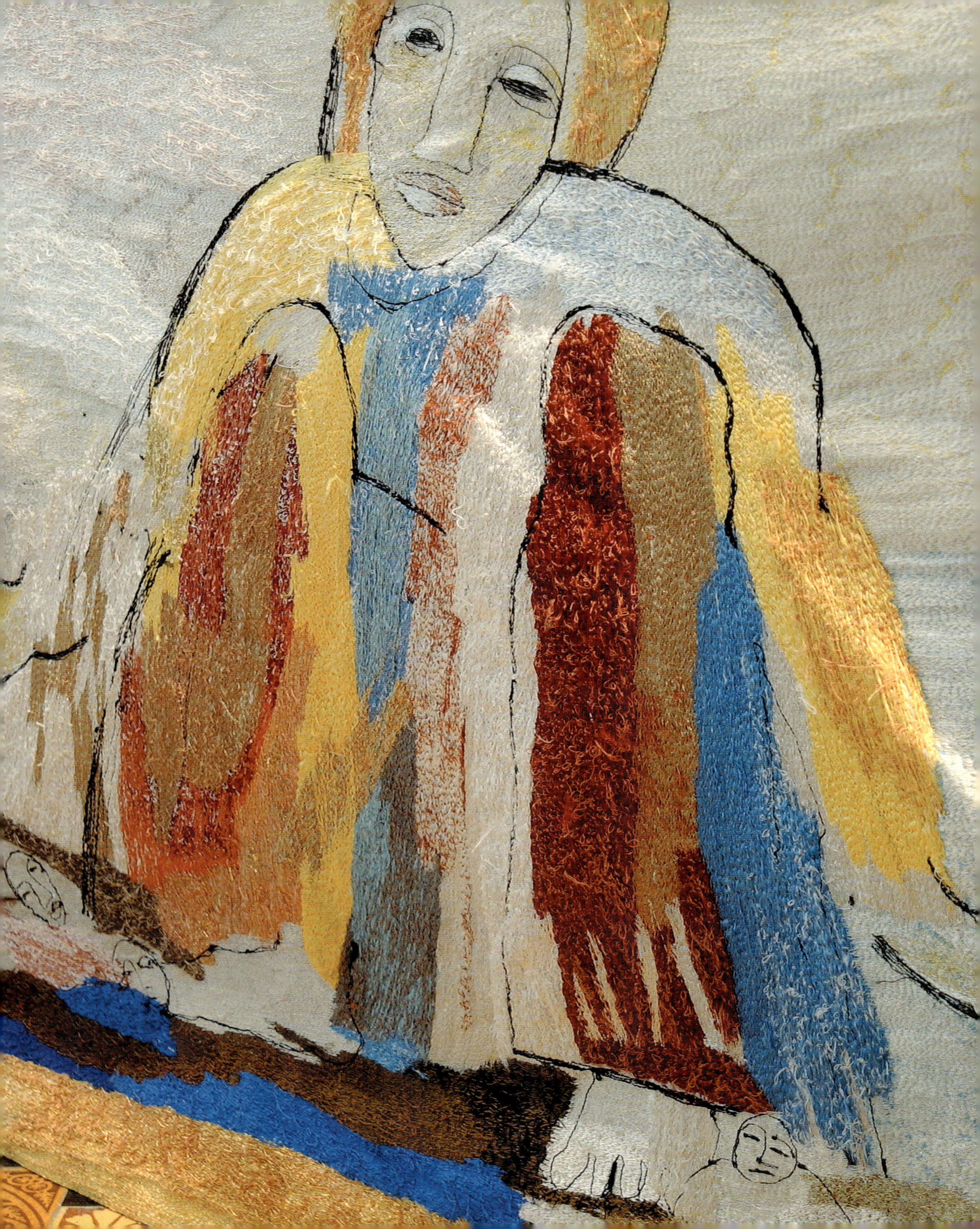

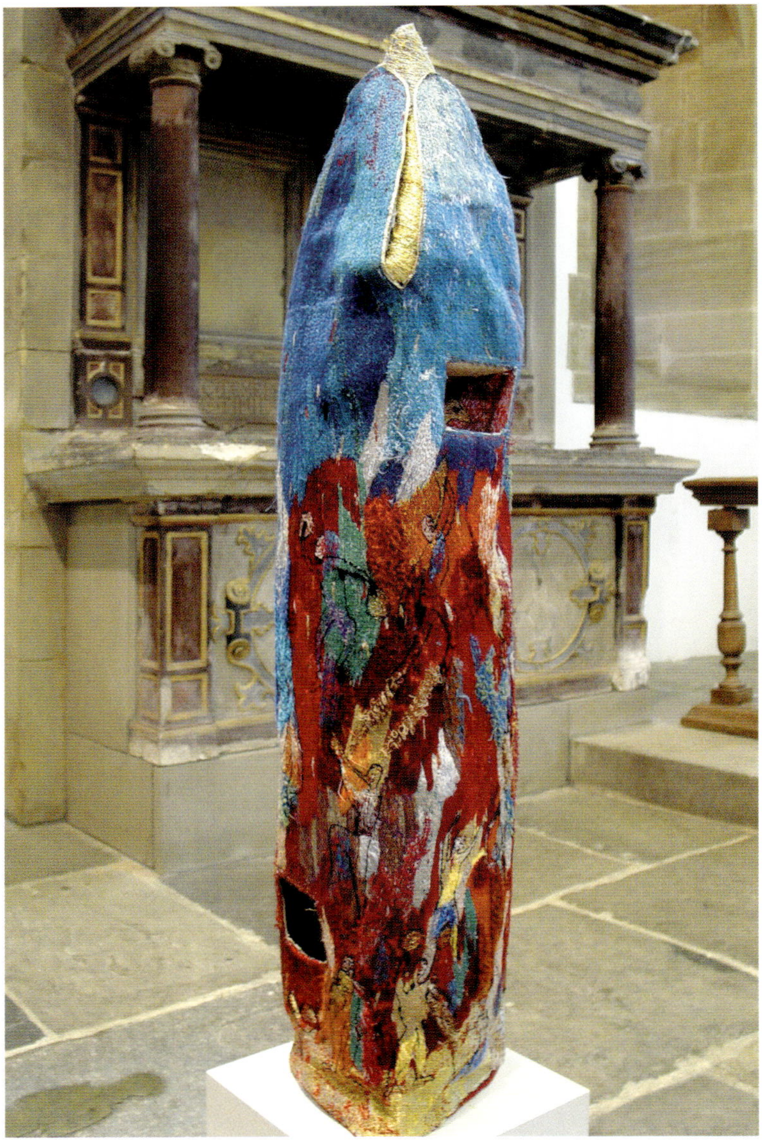

Chagall Column

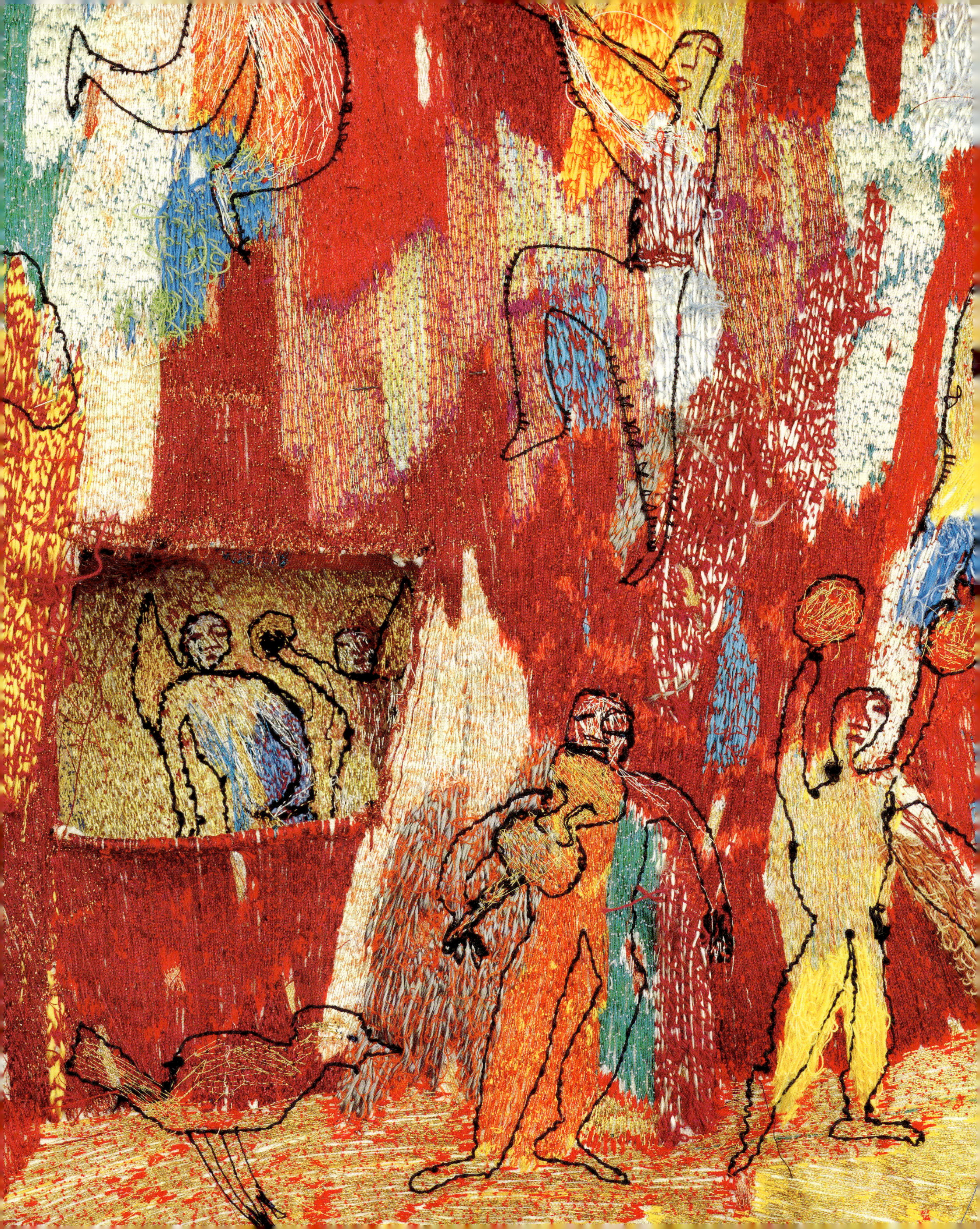

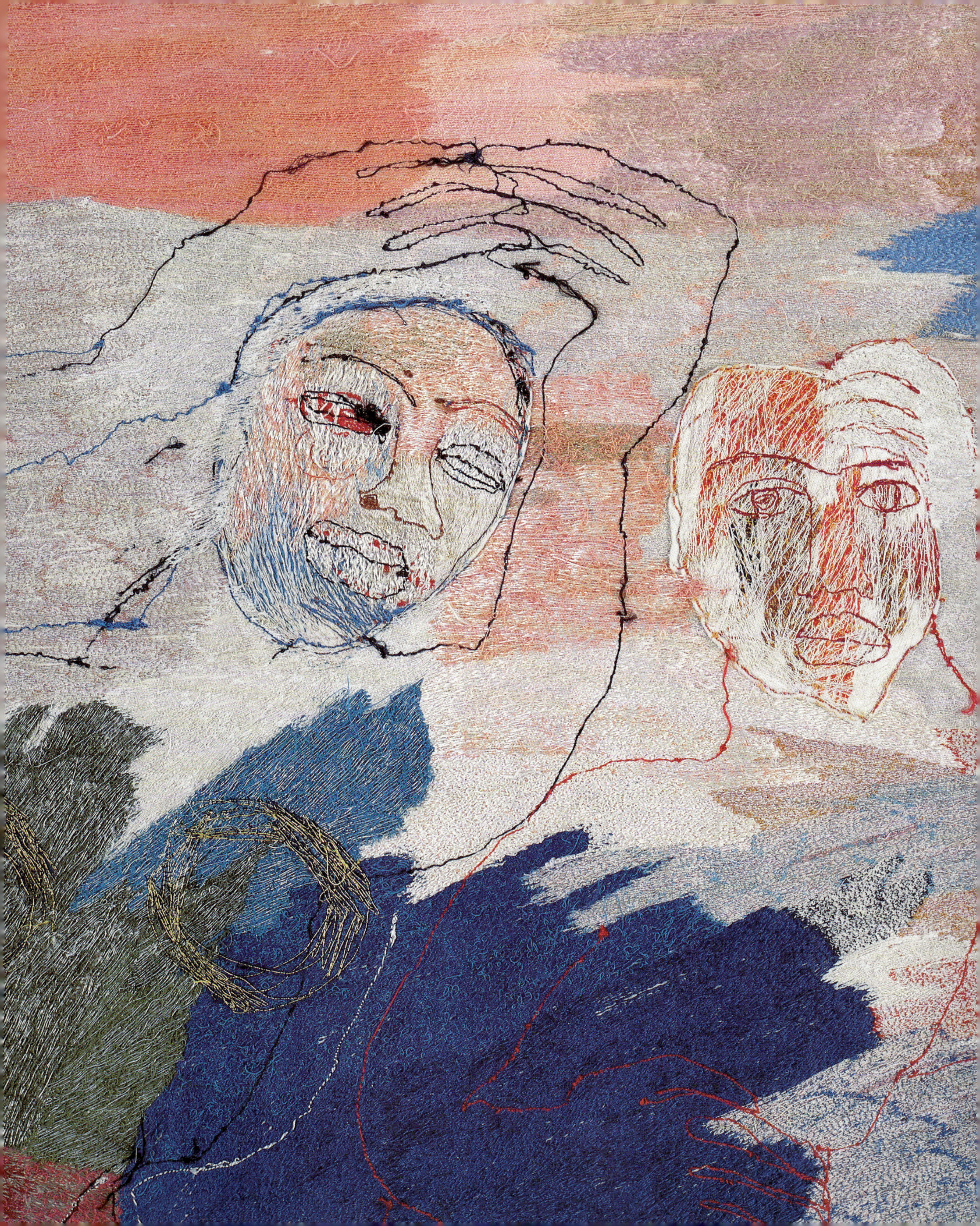

ODYSSEUS' DECISION

The great man turns his back on the island.
Now he will not die in paradise
nor hear again
the lutes of paradise among the olive trees,
by the clear pools under the cypresses. Time

begins now, in which he hears again
that pulse which is the narrative
sea, at dawn when its pull is strongest.
What has brought us here
will lead us away; our ship
sways in the tinted harbor water.

Now the spell is ended.
Give him back life,
sea that can only move forward.

CIRCE'S TORMENT

...the years of loving you in both
your presence and absence, regret
the law, the vocation
that forbid me to keep you, the sea
a sheet of glass, the sun-bleached
beauty of the Greek ships: how
could I have power if
I had no wish
to transform you:

Louise Glück

Odyssey (detail)

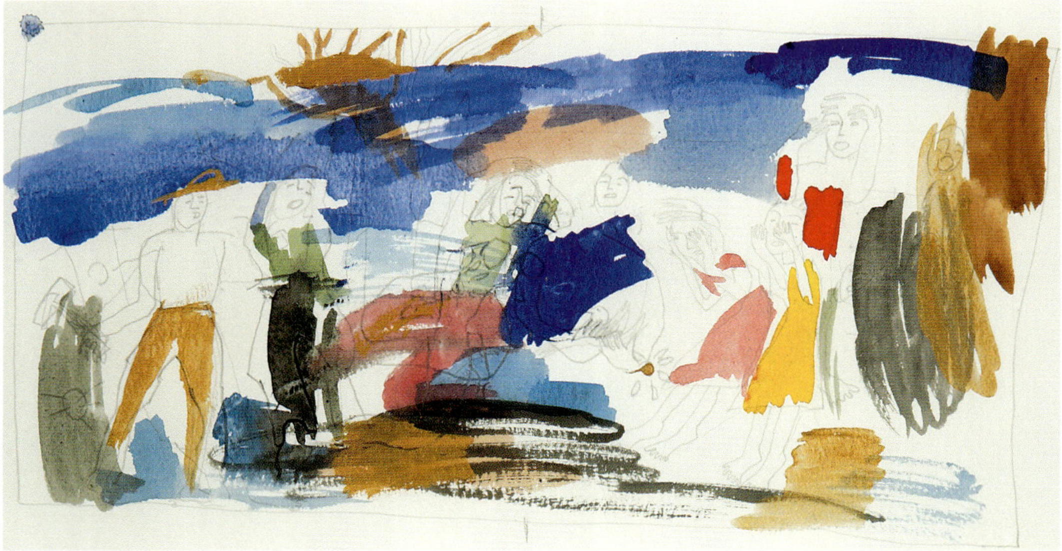

Odyssey sketch

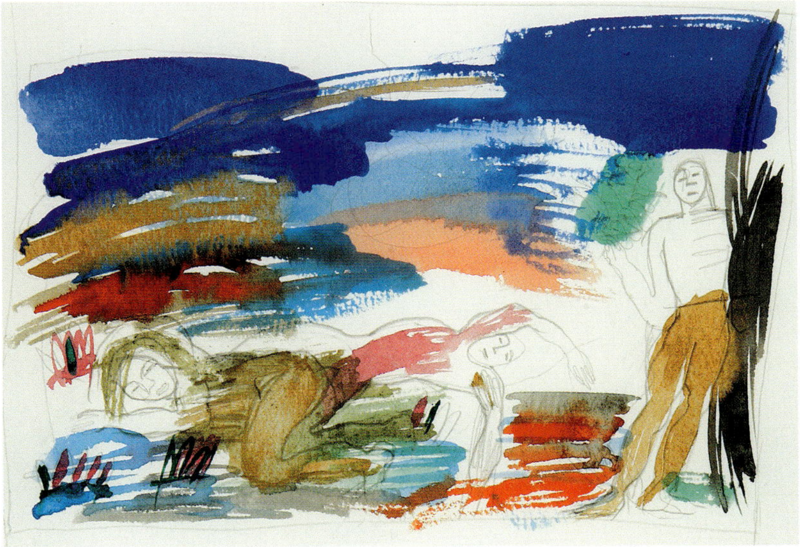

Lotos-Eaters and Hermes sketch

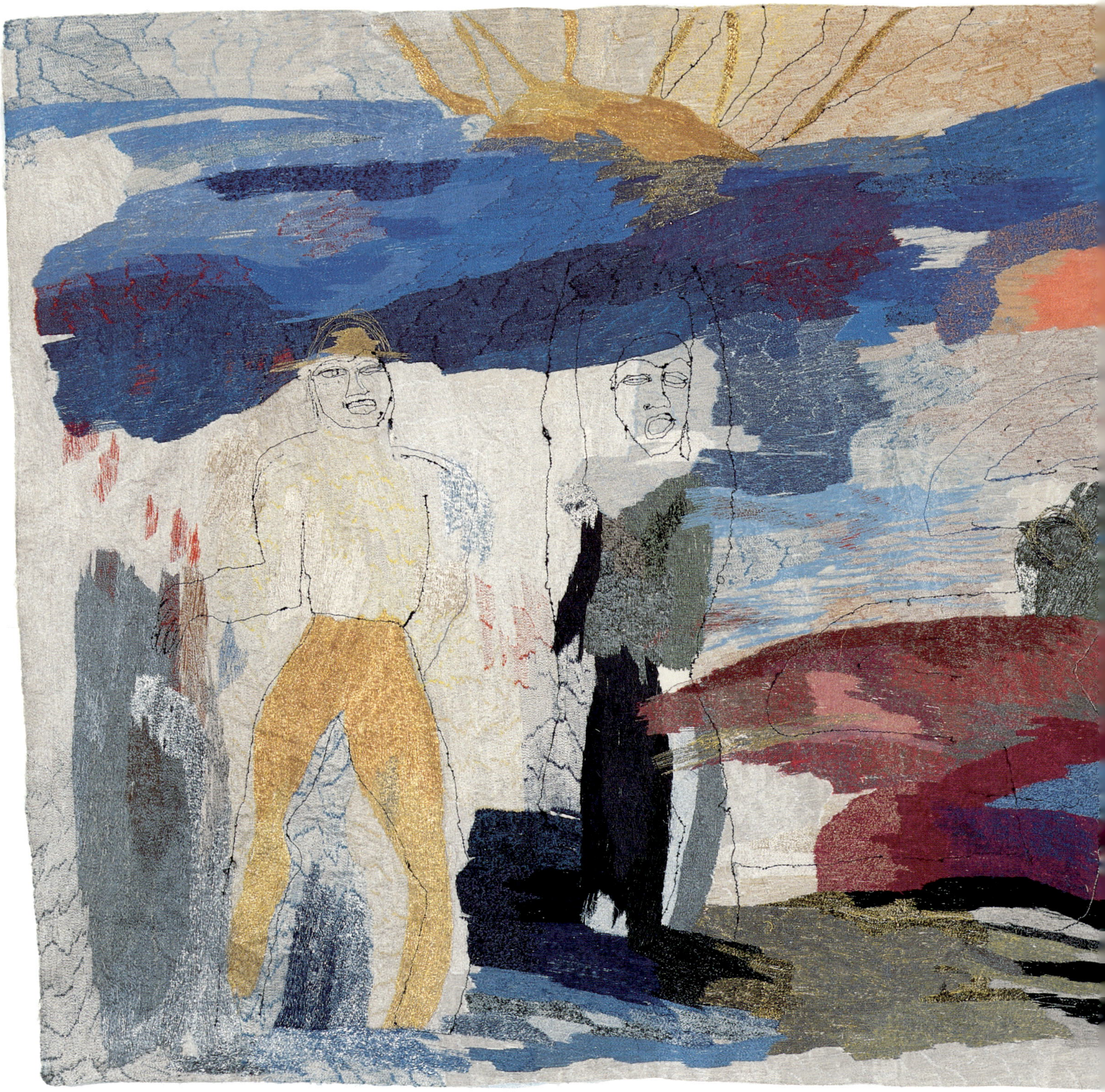

Odyssey

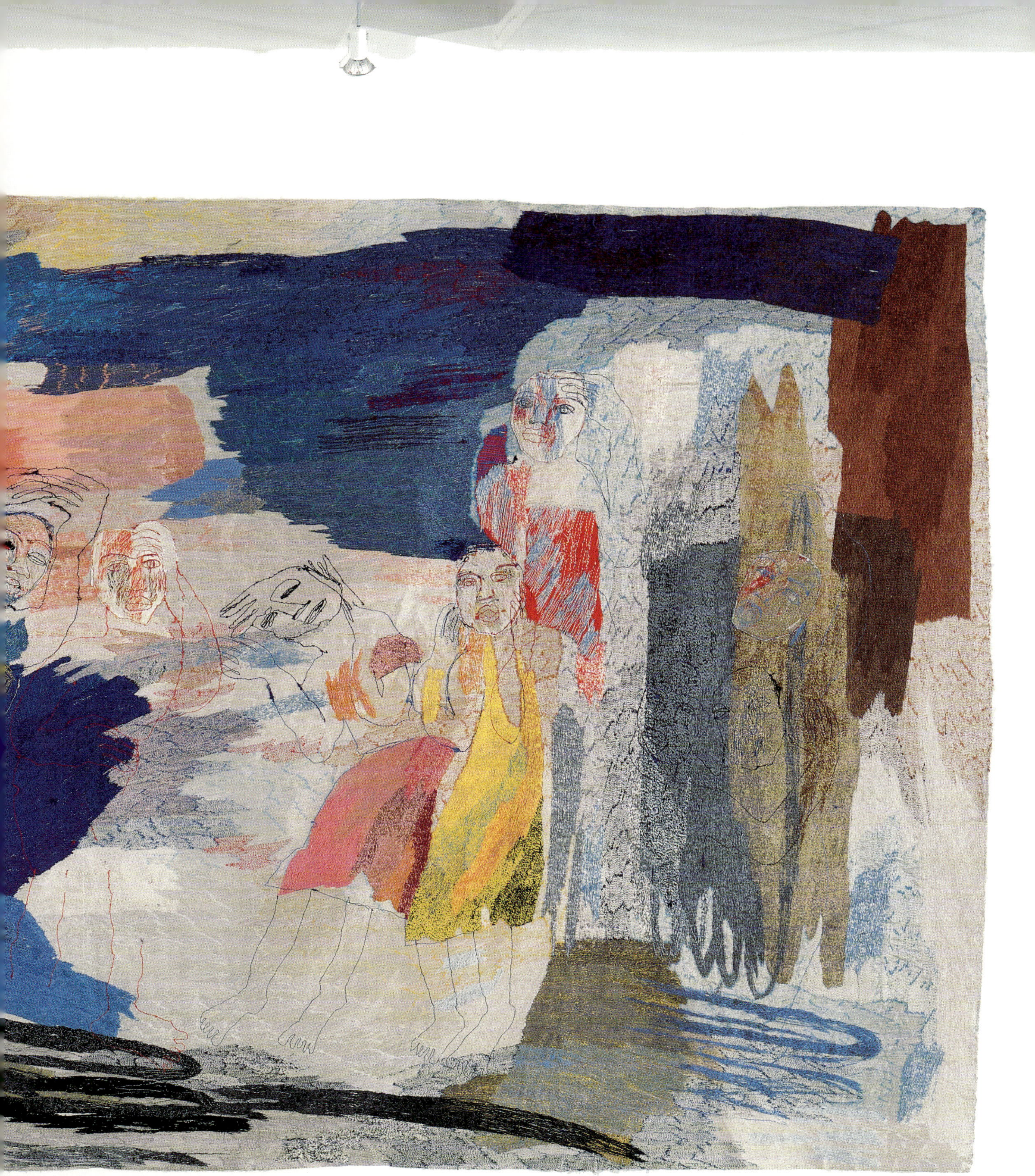

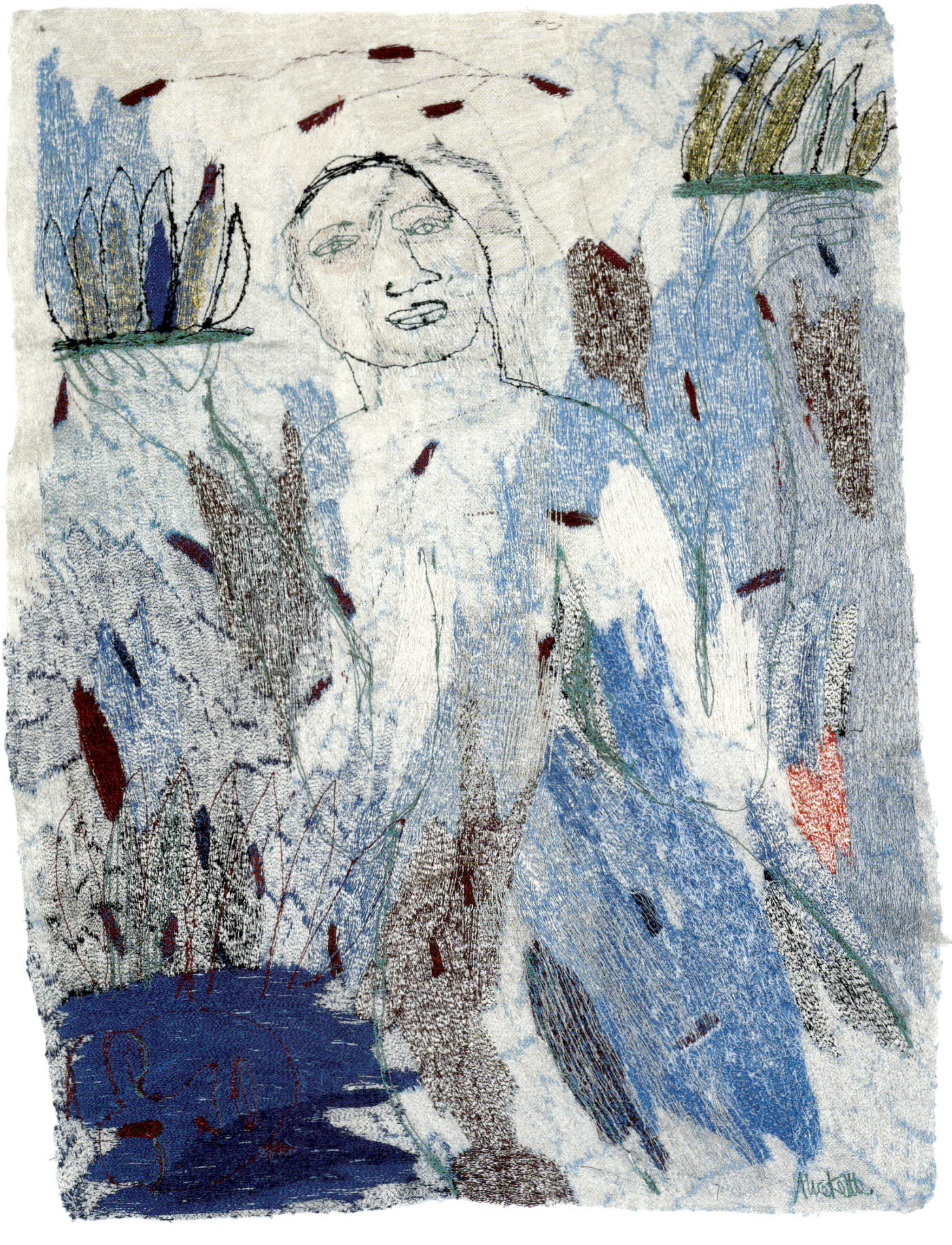

Lotos-Eaters

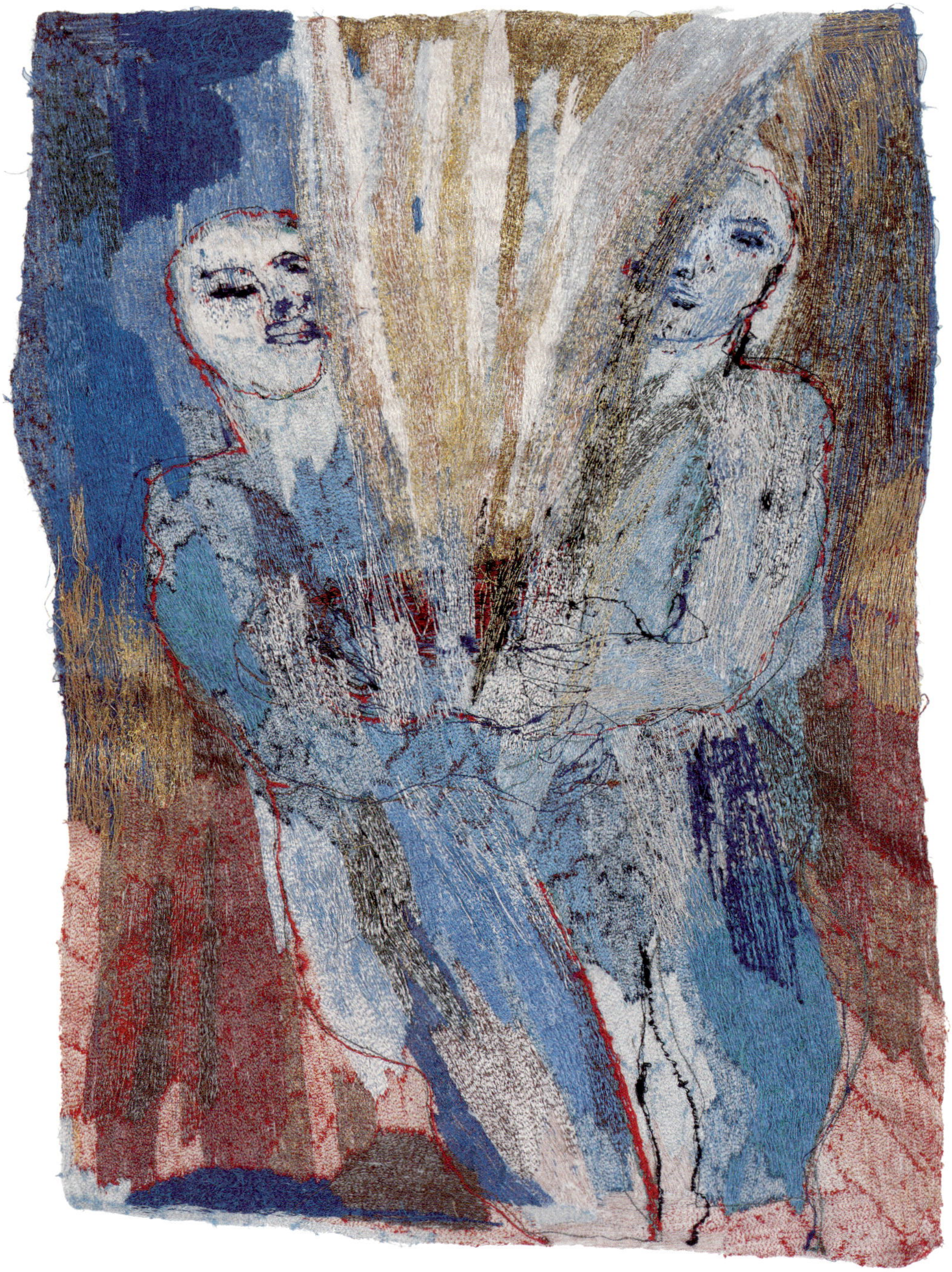

Bag of Winds

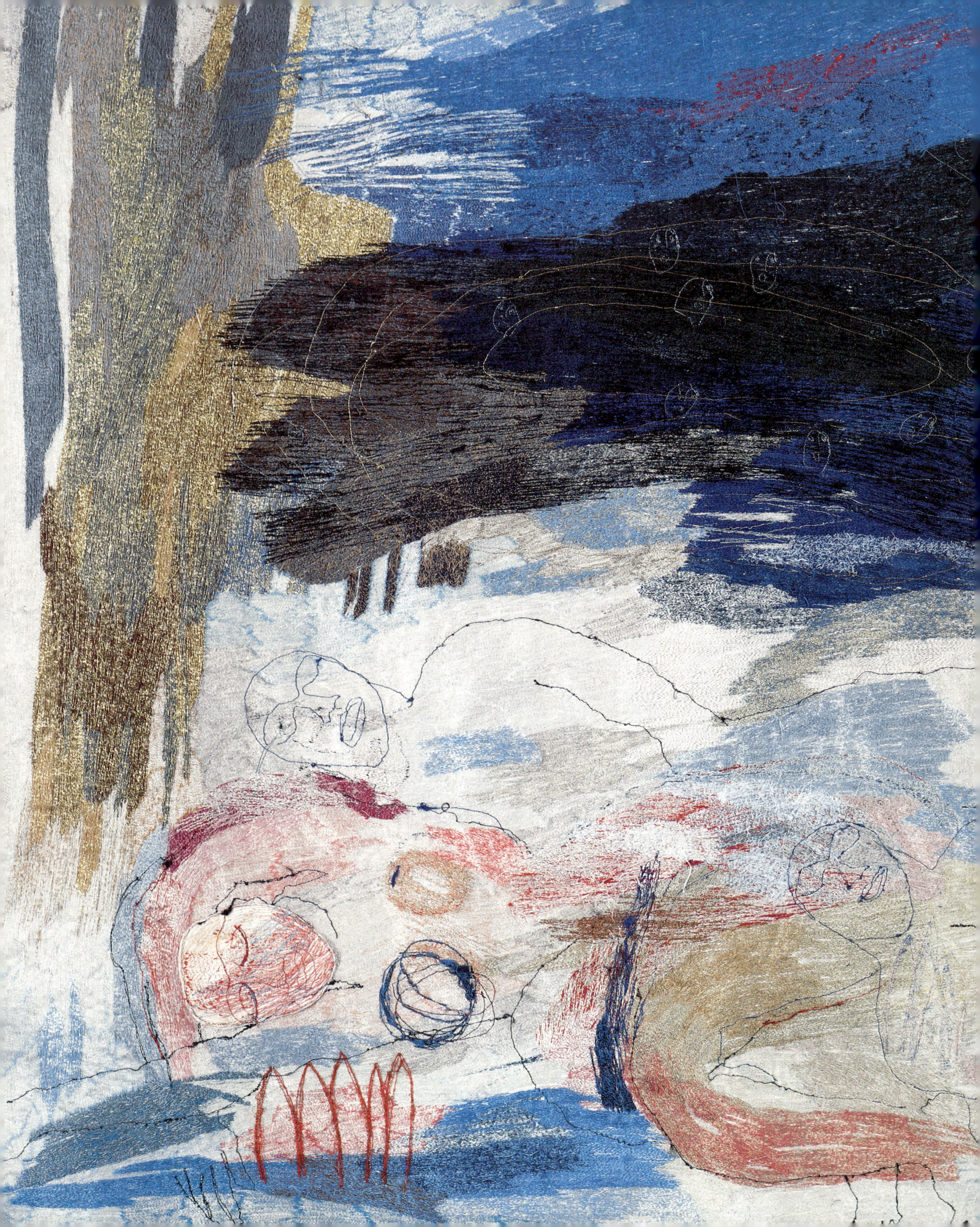

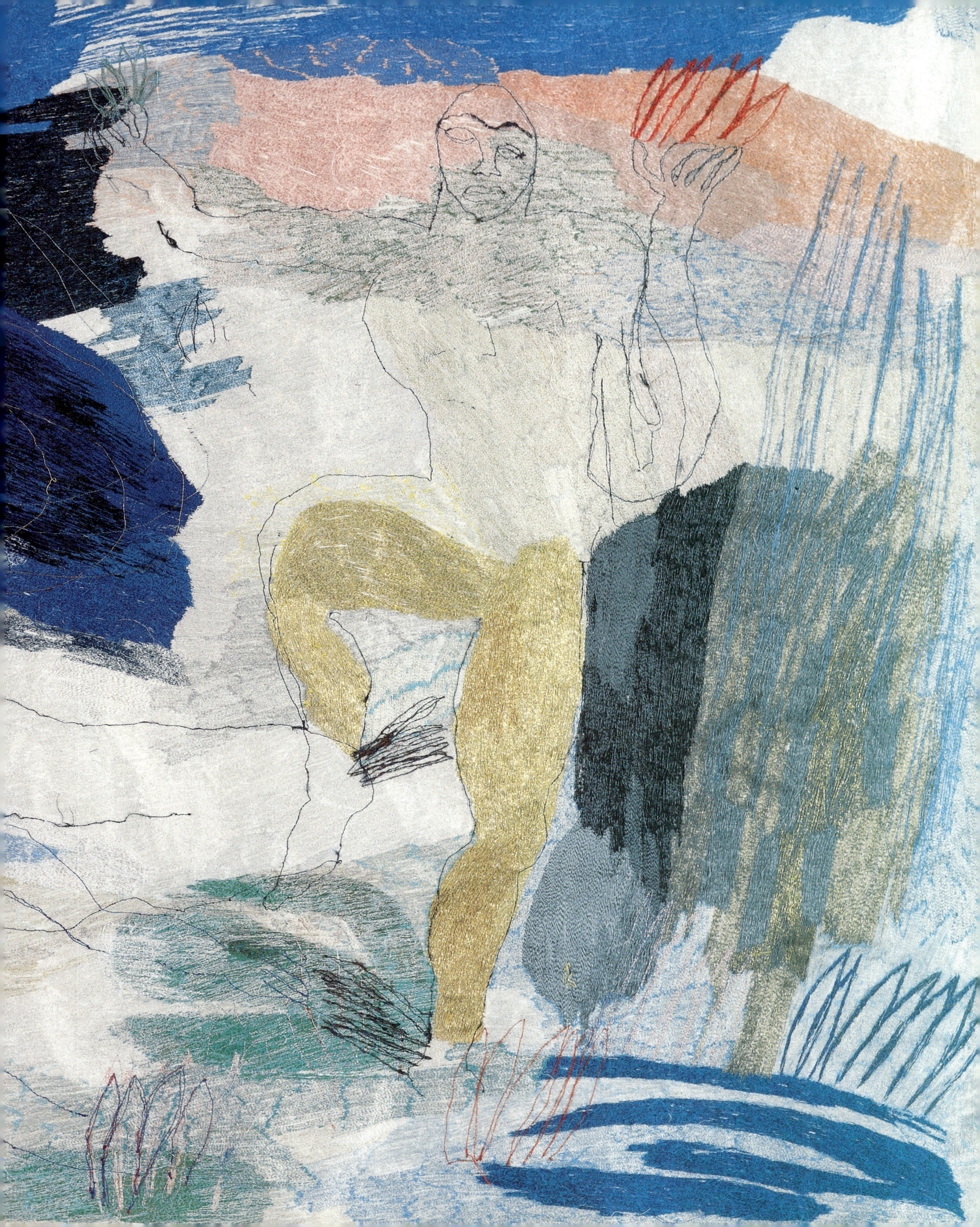

Alice Kettle: Odyssey

New narrative work

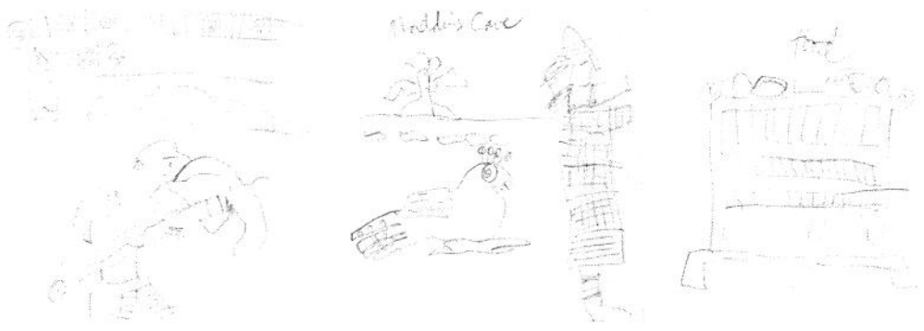

From there they could hear Circe within, singing in her beautiful voice as she went to and fro at her great and everlasting loom, on which she was weaving one of those delicate, graceful, and dazzling fabrics that goddesses love to make.
Homer 'The Odyssey'

Even to those who don't know Homer's great poem *The Odyssey* itself, the characters are familiar, we absorb them through children's stories, through references in literature, theatre and art, they are part of a shared symbolic order lodged deep in our collective culture: Circe, the goddess who turned the sailors into swine; the spaced-out Lotos-Eaters; the lumbering, terrifying Cyclops with its single eye; Scylla and Charybdis, the original 'rock and a hard place'. The poem is rich in character, imagery and plot excitement: and, appropriately for Alice Kettle, textile references: Circe's pastimes aside, for four years Odysseus' loyal wife Penelope successfully put off unwelcome suitors with the conceit that she had to complete a great textile: a shroud for her father-in-law Laertes. She prolonged her freedom to await her husband's return by intensive and deceptive endeavour: *'...by day she wove at the great web, but every night had torches set beside it and undid the work.'*

The Odyssey provides appropriate material for Alice's recent work for all these reasons and more. She is fascinated with myth and storytelling, and this story more than most allows for the exploration of emotional themes hung on an eventful epic narrative with enormous visual potential. Seeing the Victorian copy of the Bayeux Tapestry recently at Reading Museum strengthened her resolve to make a narrative work, gave her the confidence to attempt a complex story within a single piece, and influenced the format: unusually for Alice, *Odyssey (2003)* is a huge horizontal panel allowing for several scenes to be played out at once. It is epic, in a modern cinematic sense, its surface shimmering with movement. This main work is complemented by smaller satellite pieces depicting other scenes from the poem: the *Lotos-Eaters*; the goddess *Calypso*; the release of the *Bag of Winds* (all 2003). The texture and pace of Homer's *Odyssey* is reflected in part in Alice's textile: it is a dense physical substance, an intensely-worked fabric supporting narrative and particular incident. Homer's *Odyssey* uses the full metaphorical force of the journey: as a means of self-discovery through the exploration of the other, a marrying of history with new experience. The intensity of painting with stitch is, for Alice, akin to a journey: a process which transports the imagination, requiring

Sketches of the replica Bayeux Tapestry
Odyssey (detail)

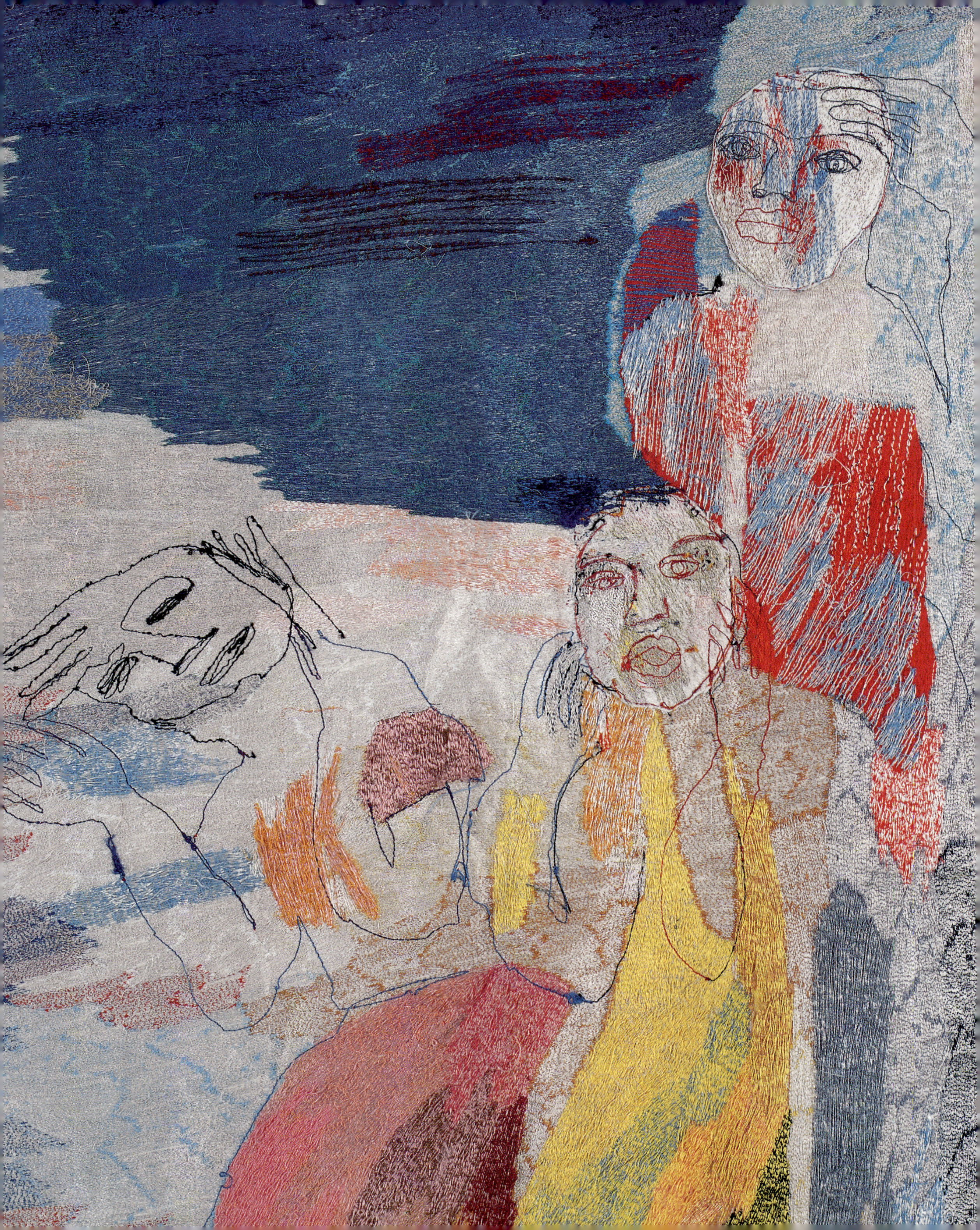

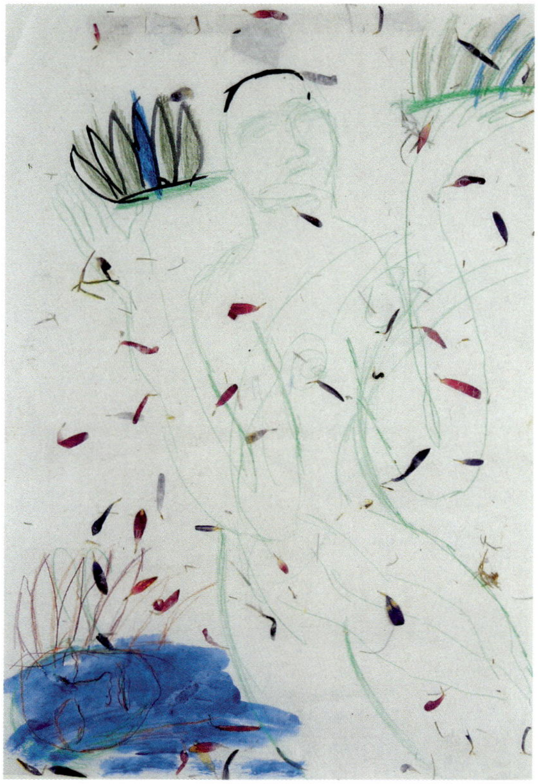

an intense mental and emotional engagement and a resolution of problems along the way. *The Odyssey* is on the one hand about retaining a sense of self, Odysseus resisting the temptations available on his journey. It is about being focussed on the main event, drawing from inner strength in the face of adversity.

Alice Kettle is an artist who has established a unique area of practice by her use of a craft medium, consistently and on an unparalleled scale. She has extended the possibilities of machine embroidery: producing works the size of tapestries, exploiting the textures and effects made possible through the harnessing of a mechanical process to intuitive, creative ends. The scale of her works belies their component parts: individual tiny stitches which combine to form great swathes of colour, painterly backgrounds incorporating rich hues and metallic sheen. Before her time at Goldsmiths' Textile department, and while studying Fine Art at Reading, she began making non-figurative abstract expressionist paintings, influenced by visiting tutor Albert Irvin and Reader at Reading, Terry Frost. She has carried this bold confidence with colour and composition into her figurative works, and indeed at the stage of their construction before the figures are introduced, these might be large colour-field works, one panel of colour reacting with its neighbour in a vibrant expressive whole.

It is revealing, however, that her acknowledged influences are sculptural. Asked to name them, she recalls the effect of very particular pieces: Matisse's weighty studies of backs; and, in contrast, Flanagan's hares for their levity, their vigour, their presence as drawings in space; Richard Long for his 'virtuous putting together of materials'; Antony Gormley's figure *Sound II* (1989) in the partially-flooded crypt of Winchester Cathedral, for its emotive use of human scale; a Henry Moore exhibition seen in the Museum of Modern Art in Greece, massive figurative forms displayed against the background of the sea; Epstein's vast alabaster Jacob and the Angel, ("Wouldn't it be wonderful to have a huge supporting angel like that?"). The real influence of these monumental figurative pieces is manifest in her

Lotos-Eaters sketch
Odyssey (detail)

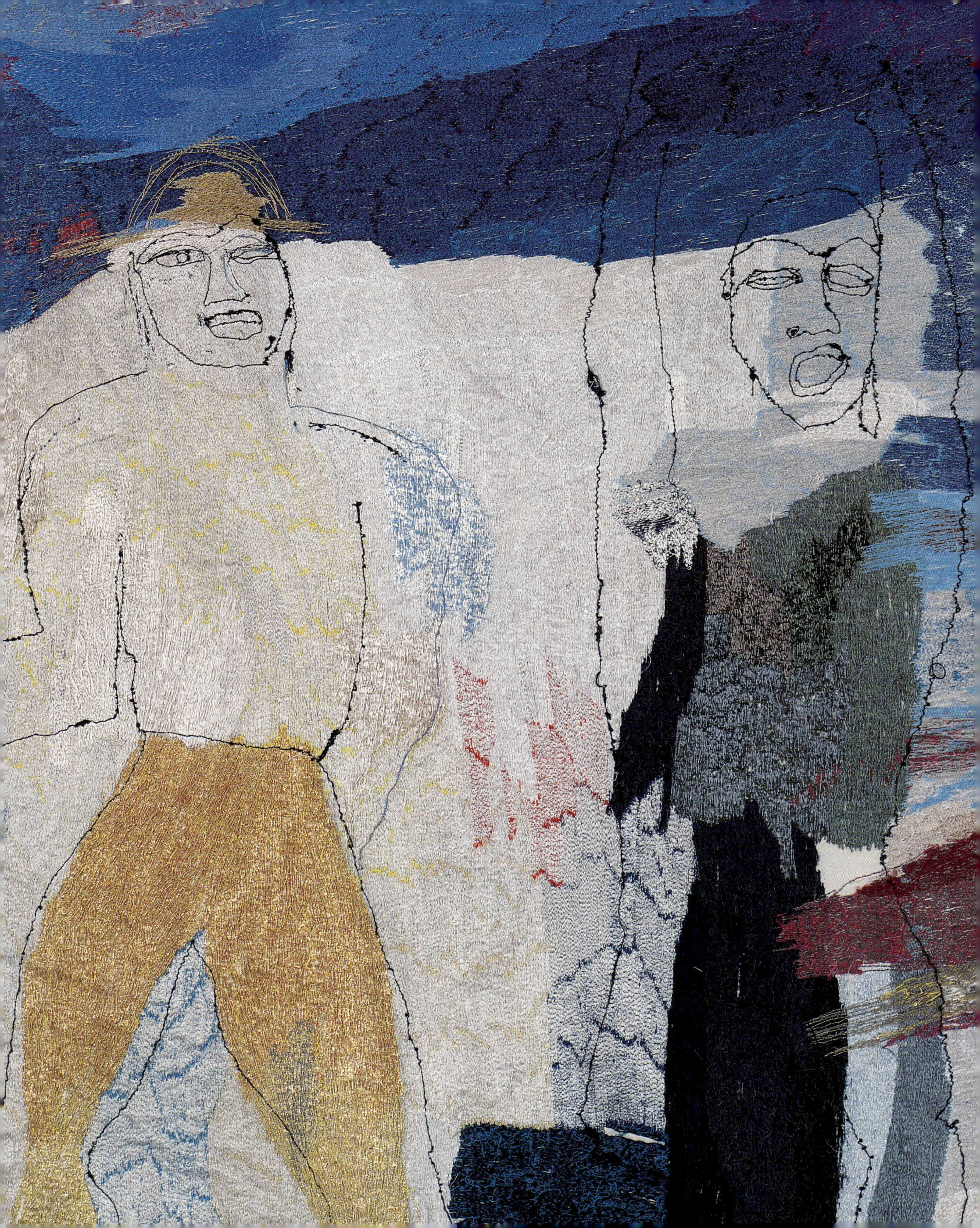

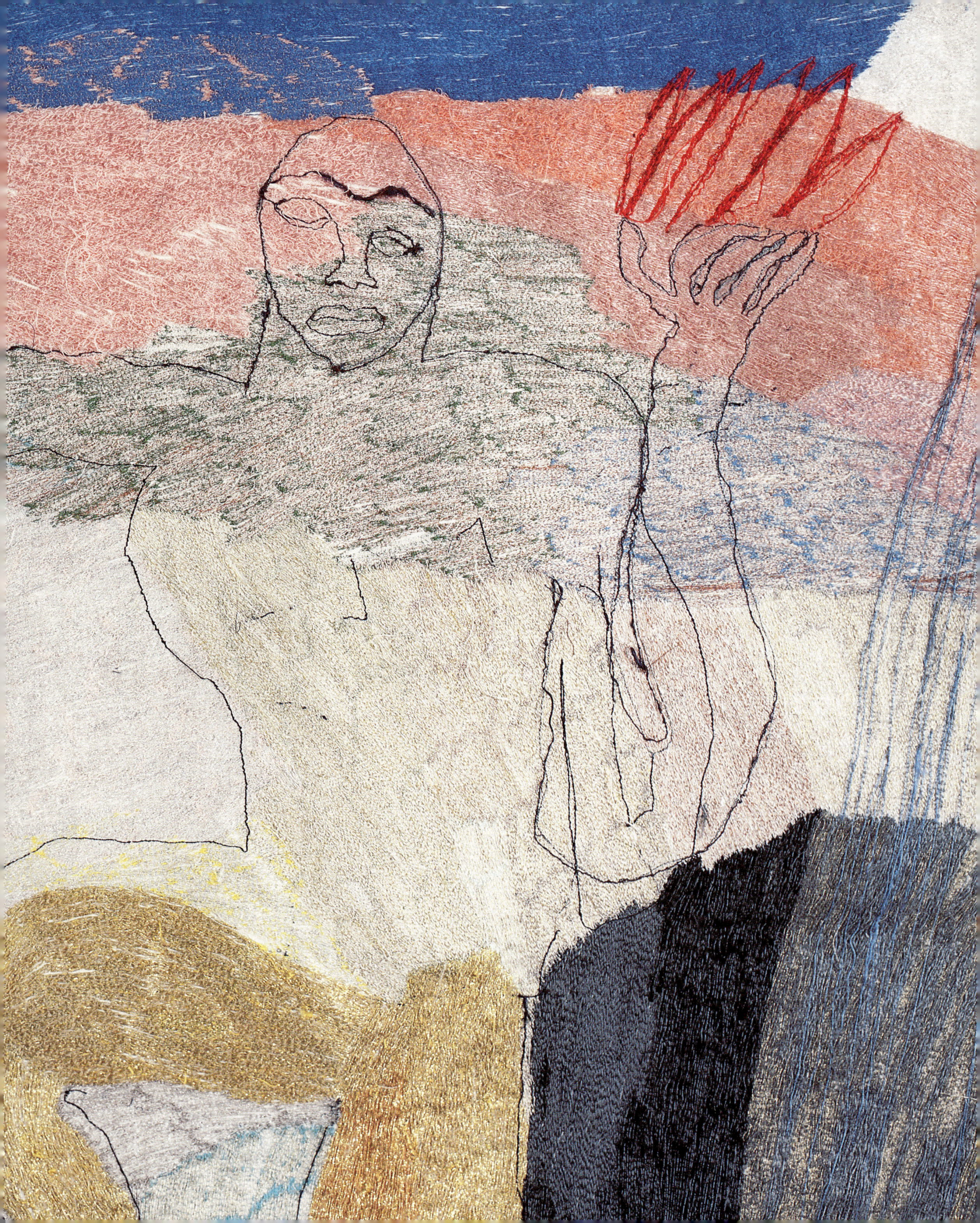

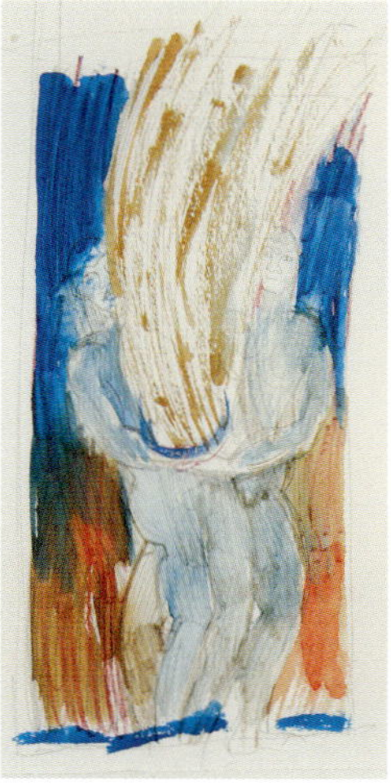

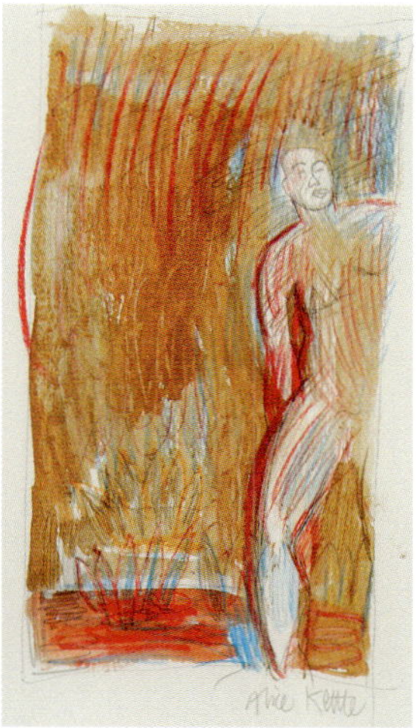

latest works. Her earlier figures, such as *Harlequin Madonna* (1986) and *Eve Falling from Grace* (1986), occupy an ethereal space unaffected by gravity or the forces of their own weight: they adopt poses determined by the parameters of the textile edge, but float upon the background, merging with it like the figures in a Klimt painting, a mosaic of decorative marks. Her recent figures are more weighty, they look as if they occupy real space, they are grounded: the several figures in the *Odyssey* are more substantial, more believable, their features fully resolved. Whilst some are line drawings, some are heavily worked and reworked tonal renditions. This gives rhythm within the figures, establishes their relationships and helps distinguish the main protagonists in the narrative.

This body of work marks a return to classical themes following a series of prestigious commissions through the 1990s. It is distinguished not only by a new confidence in depiction of the figure, but also by an enhanced relationship between painting and drawing through stitch. Of late her drawing has become more assertive, with a new assuredness of line as well as of mass. She speaks of the process of laying down colours as meditative, a partly detached state which controls and allows an outpouring of emotion: but this intense process is also all-consuming, noisy and physically very demanding due to the scale of the work being manipulated. Months of this concerted repetitive effort finally give way to the charge of excitement at suddenly changing pace: drawing with stitch is the climax of the creative process, a liberating release. Because of the thickness of the textile, its enormous bulk, and to achieve the stitch effects she desires, Alice frequently draws 'blind' from the back of the work, an edgy, risk-taking element. Like Penelope, she constructs and deconstructs, unafraid to cut through areas representing months of labour in order to reconfigure a work, to erase and occasionally unpick stitched line and to redraw repeatedly. But traces remain: the evidence of these layers of thinking is apparent in the finished work, showing that meaning lies not only in the product but in the process.

The tension inherent in their surfaces and their own weight cause her textiles to take up wavy forms, and Alice has always has always been interested in the way that this gives objects which are obviously hangings an animated relationship with the wall. She first exaggerated this natural consequence of her technique in *Creation* (1991): it is suspended from shaped profiles on the wall which bulk out the panels and emphasise their columnar shape. *Creation* is an

Lotos-Eaters and Hermes (detail)
Bag of Winds sketch
Man sketch

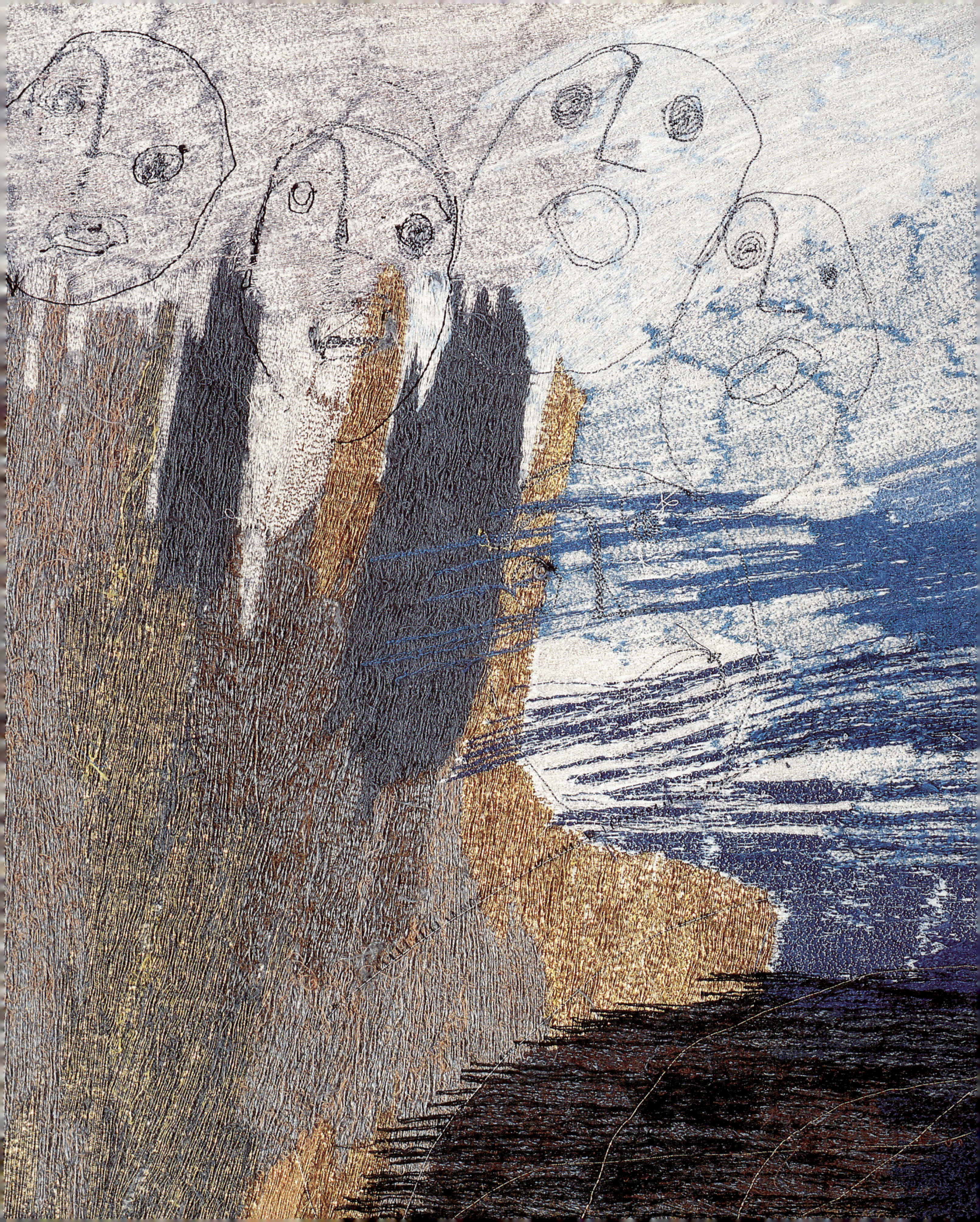

PENELOPE

In the pathway of the sun,
In the footsteps of the breeze,
Where the world and sky are one,
He shall ride the silver seas,
He shall cut the glittering wave.
I shall sit at home, and rock;
Rise to heed a neighbour's knock;
Brew my tea, and snip my thread;
Bleach the linen for my bed.
They will call him brave.

Dorothy Parker

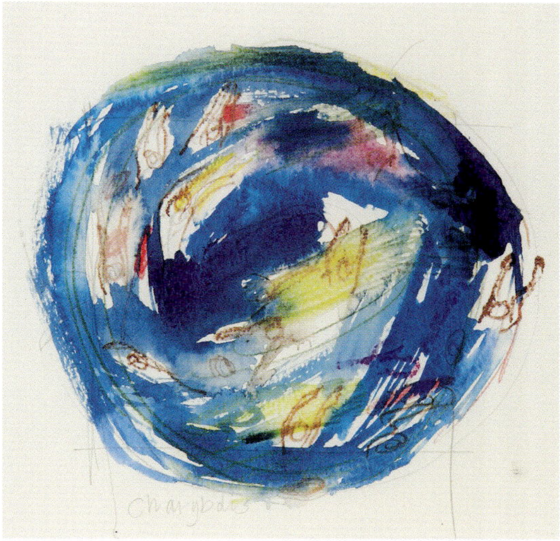

image of humanity in its nascent, purest form. Calm, filled with light, it celebrates the pure potential of human life. *Towers* (2002) marks the other end of the scale, a work made in shocked reaction to the events of September 11 2001. It is document of human suffering, a man-made disaster of previously unimagined proportion: one panel of the triptych has seemingly collapsed, its mass falling in great folds onto the floor. This very physical aspect of her work is now being even more closely linked with the subject matter it describes. In the *Odyssey* series, *Scylla and Charybdis* (2003) are columnar and pool-like respectively, the distorted features of drowning sailors crumpled and redrawn on the peaks of textile waves, their misery drawn in deep relief.

Alice has found, in *The Odyssey*, a bountiful seam of material with which to work: it is rich visual territory; it deals with grand themes; it is about longing and searching; it is expressive of so many human truths. Her *Odyssey* is ambitious both in its scale and its range, an epic work peopled by fully-developed interacting characters. It would have made an extraordinary painting, but the fact of its rich, dense fabric further emphasises its power and substance. Appropriately, Homer's *Odyssey* supports not only a hero in Odysseus, retaining his primary objective throughout a long and eventful journey; but also a powerful heroine, Penelope, whose outward vulnerability belies great strength, and who keeps faith by weaving and unweaving.

Sara Roberts

Lotos-Eaters and Hermes (detail)
Charybdis sketch

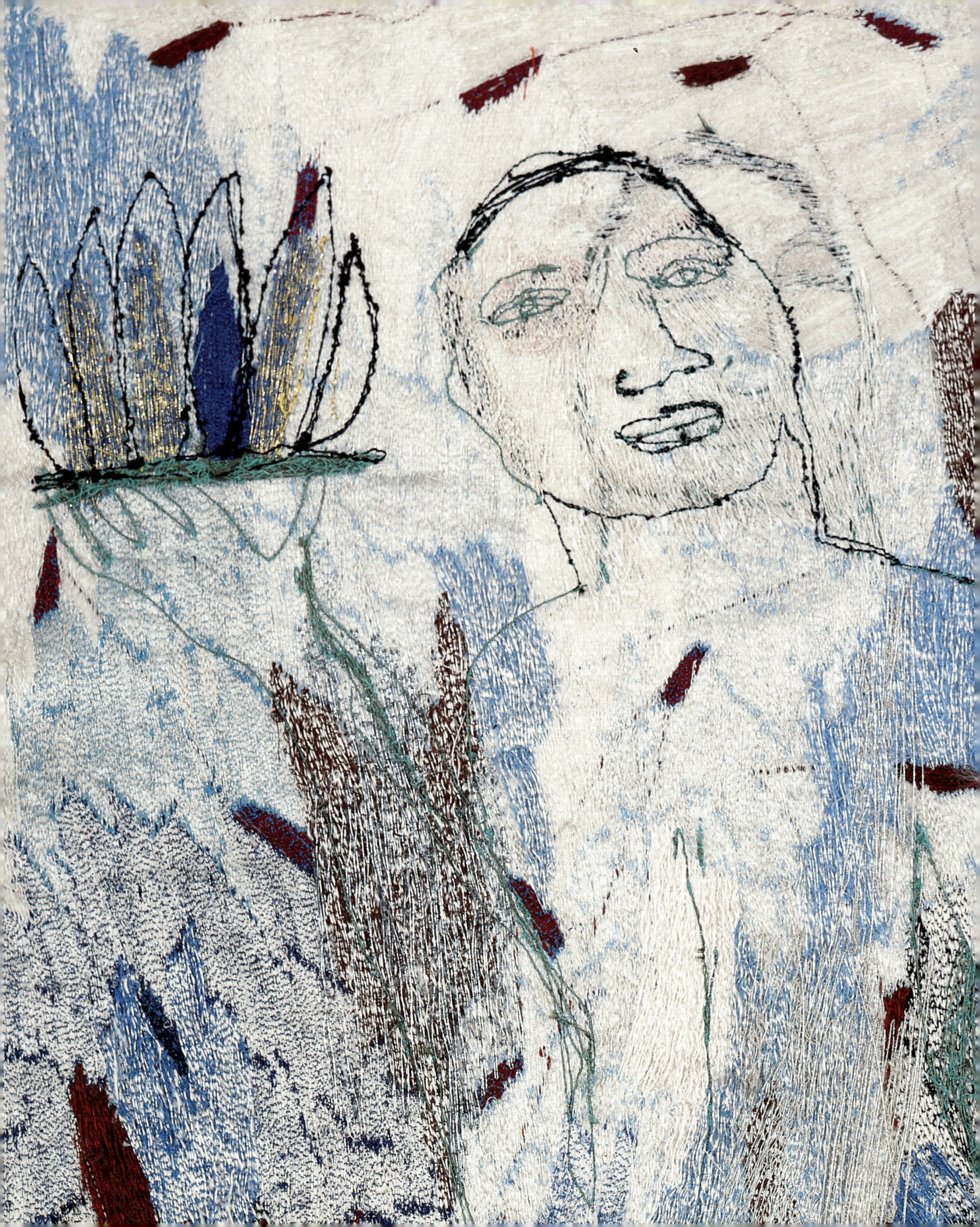

SONG OF THE LOTOS-EATERS

There is sweet music here that softer falls
Than petals from blown roses on the grass,
Or night-dews on still waters between walls
Of shadowy granite, in a gleaming pass;
Music that gentlier on the spirit lies,
than tired eyelids upon tired eyes;
Music that brings sweet sleep down from the blissful skies.
Here cool mosses deep,
And through the moss the ivies creep,
And in the stream the long-leaved flowers weep,
And from the craggy ledge the poppy hangs in sleep.

Why are we weighed upon with heaviness,
And utterly consumed with sharp distress,
While all things else have rest from weariness?
All things have rest: why should we toil alone,
We only toil, who are the first of things,
And make perpetual moan,
Still from one sorrow to another thrown:
Nor ever fold our wings,
And cease from wanderings,
Nor steep our brows in slumber's holy balm;
Nor harken what the inner spirit sings,
'There is no joy but calm!'
Why should we toil, the roof and crown of things?

Alfred, Lord Tennyson

Lotos-Eaters (detail)

Thoughts on Alice Kettle

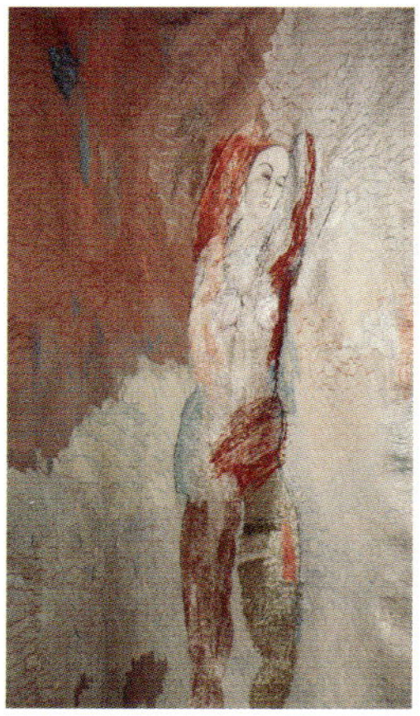

The Three Caryatids

In 1992 the Gallery had only recently begun to collect textile art and the 'Caryatids' represented a major purchase in what was then still an emerging discipline. External funders as well as Gallery staff had to be persuaded of their significance and brought on board to make the purchase possible. Raising the necessary funds and seeing the work acquire almost iconic status gave me confidence as a curator. It convinced me to go with 'gut' instinct when acquiring new art. The 'wow' factor of Three Caryatids remains absolutely undimmed and they are always in the Top Ten of our visitors' favourite works.

Jennifer Harris
Deputy Director
Whitworth Art Gallery

Chagall Column

I first met Alice Kettle's work at University College Chichester, where we have her Harlequin Madonna (1986). The beauty of this work led me to ask Alice to think of a piece in three-dimensions – to celebrate the Chagall windows both at Chichester Cathedral and at Tudeley in Kent, about which I was then writing. Alice's response was immediate and supremely creative, and demonstrates what I can only call her poetic imagination. It was Coleridge who said that the imagination has the power to synthesize in a magical way; and this is exactly what Alice Kettle can achieve. Her work is poetic – in the best sense of the word: it unifies a huge variety of impulses and resources in a whole that excites the sensibility and invigorates the mind. She is a true artist.

Professor Paul Foster
University College
Chichester

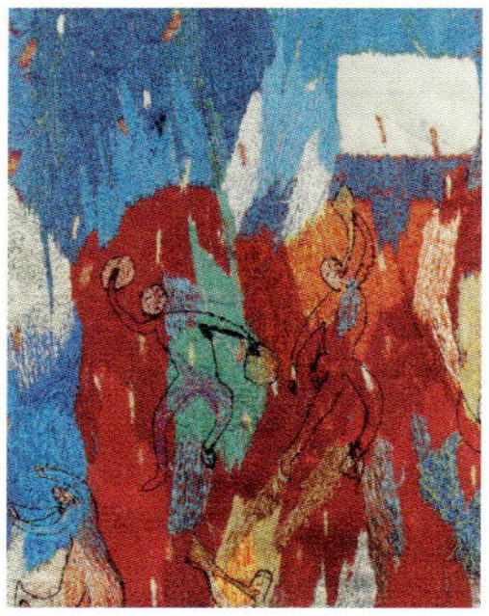

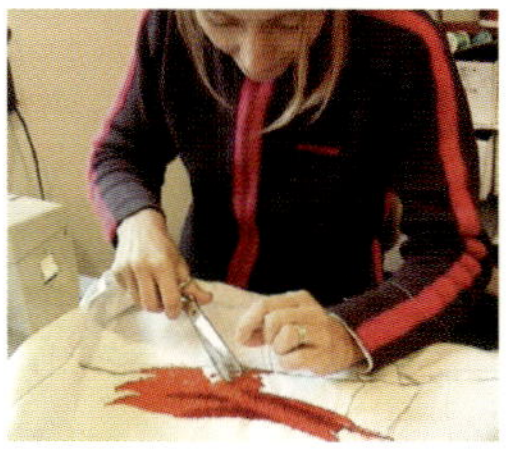

Studio work

When I first met Alice at the beginning of her career in her studio in Winchester, the painterly beauty and innovative quality of her work was impressive. Time has shown that she is an artist whose work continues to challenge the boundaries of what is possible. Recognition of her achievement through this exhibition is richly deserved.

David Kay
Freelance Arts Consultant
Formerly Craft Officer with Southern Arts

Winchester Cathedral

The textile work of Alice Kettle maintains the highest standards of her burgeoning art. She has sunk deep roots into the wonders of medieval painting but has been attentive to all that modern art has to offer in terms of form and composition. Her vision is lyrical, feminine and profoundly spiritual; her expression is a highly evolved individuality, painting in thread, but with total respect for her particular medium. The altar cloth she created for the Holy Sepulchre Chapel in Winchester Cathedral shows remarkable humility respecting the 12th century wall paintings immediately behind it, but blends with their colours and form admirably. Alice's work is created to last, as textile and as composition.

Canon Keith Walker
of Winchester Cathedral

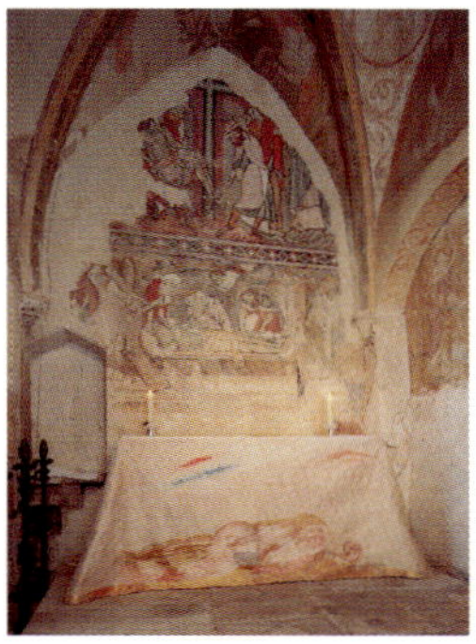

Curriculum Vitae

Born 1961 Winchester

Training

1985–86 Goldsmiths' College Postgraduate Diploma in Textile Art
1979–84 University of Reading BA Hons Fine Art

Selected Commissions

2004–05 School of Music and Drama, Manchester University
2004 Calderdale MBC: Museums and Arts
2001 Chagall Column, Professor Paul Foster
1999–01 Three altar frontals for the High Altar, Gloucester Cathedral
1999–00 The National Library of Australia, Canberra, Australia
1995–97 In Camera, High Court, Lawnmarket, Edinburgh
1995 Grandeur of the Seas, Royal Caribbean Cruise Lines
1994 Altar frontal, Holy Sepulchre Chapel, Winchester Cathedral
1994–95 Glimpses of India, MV Oriana, P&O Cruises
1992 Overtures of Gold, Open University Faculty of Arts
1991 The Saga of McGuiness Dog, Southern Arts

Various private commissions

Solo Exhibitions

2004–06 Solo touring exhibition: Bankfield Museum, Halifax; (catalogue)
mac, Birmingham;
The Gallery, Ruthin Craft Centre;
Southampton City Art Gallery;
Hove Museum and Art Gallery;
Brewery Arts, Kendal;
South Hill Park Arts Centre, Ringmead, Bracknell;
Cheltenham Art Gallery and Museum;
Myles Meehan Gallery, Darlington;
Harley Gallery, Worksop
2002 Newbury Spring Festival
1992 Salisbury Playhouse
1991 Galerie Filambule, Lausanne, Switzerland
1990 My Eyes, Your Hands, Brewery Arts Centre, Kendal
1990 Scottish Gallery, Edinburgh
1988 Alice Kettle – Showcase, ICA, London
1988 Oxford Gallery
1988 Quay Arts Centre, Newport, Isle of Wight

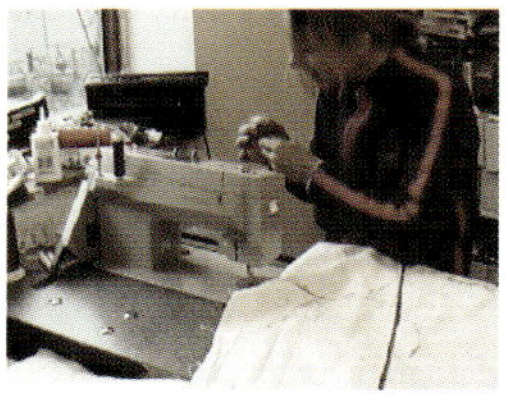

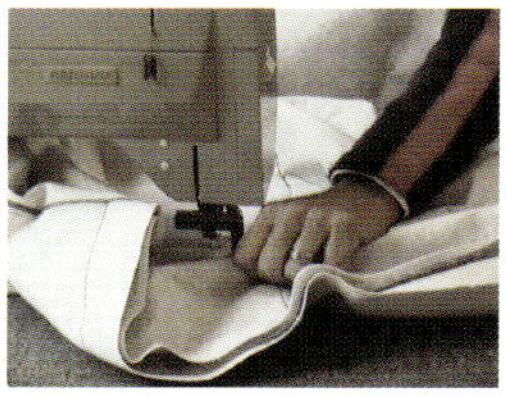

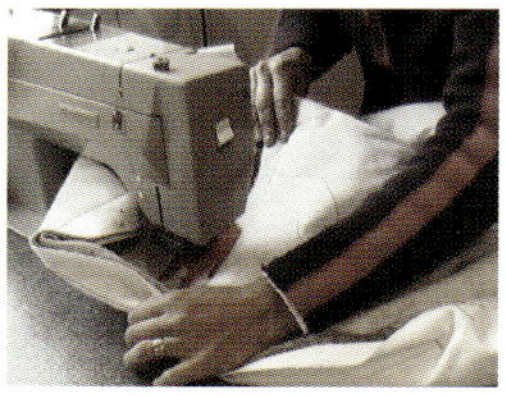

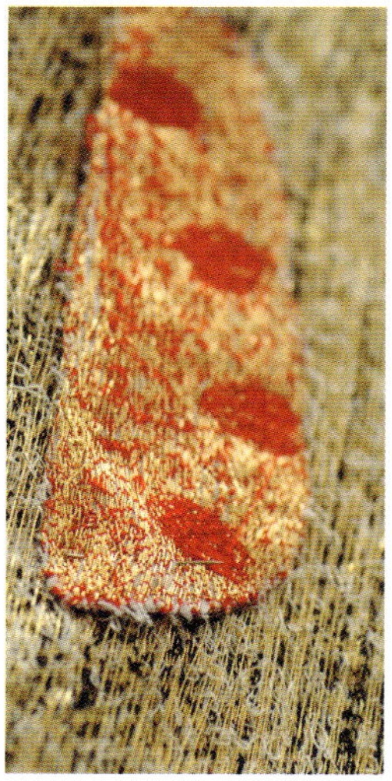

1987	University College Chichester
1987	Painting and Textiles, Oxford Gallery
1986	Oxford Gallery

Selected Exhibitions

2003	The Knitting and Stitching Show, London, Dublin and Harrogate
2003	Prism, Opus School of Textiles, Mall Galleries, London
2003	Masterpieces, International exhibition, Palazzo Bricherasio, Turin, Italy (catalogue)
2002–03	Hand to Eye, consortium of Making it Work, The Winchester Gallery and Southern Arts Visual Index Projects, touring exhibition; (catalogue) Bedales Gallery, Petersfield; The Winchester Gallery; South Hill Park, Bracknell; Oxfordshire Museum, Woodstock; Russell-Cotes Museum, Bournemouth; Reading Museum
2002	62 Group Retrospective, The Knitting and Stitching Show, London, Dublin and Harrogate
2001	Goldsmiths' Retrospective: The Knitting and Stitching Show, London, Dublin and Harrogate
2000	5th In Our Hands International competition, Kyoto, Japan (catalogue)
2000	The Unexpected, Fairfield City Museum and Stein Gallery, Sydney
1999	Art of the Stitch, Barbican Centre, London (tour) (catalogue)
1998	Knot as They Seam, Maryland Art Place, Baltimore, USA (catalogue)
1998	Cloths of Gold, Contemporary Applied Arts 50th Anniversary Exhibition
1998	Stitch, Bury St Edmunds Art Gallery
1998	The Otter Art Gallery, University College Chichester
1997	UK Now, Melbourne, Australia
1996	William Morris Revisited, Whitworth Art Gallery, Manchester, touring exhibition; (catalogue) Crafts Council, London; Birmingham City Museum and Art Gallery
1996	Hipòtesi Gallery, Barcelona
1996	Scottish Gallery, Edinburgh
1995	Art in Action, Waterperry House, Oxford (catalogue)
1995	Decorative Arts Today, Bonhams, London (also 93/92)
1995	Quarry Bank Mill, Styal
1994	Decorative Arts Today, Bonhams, London (catalogue)
1994	Northguild Gallery Shop, Southampton Civic Centre

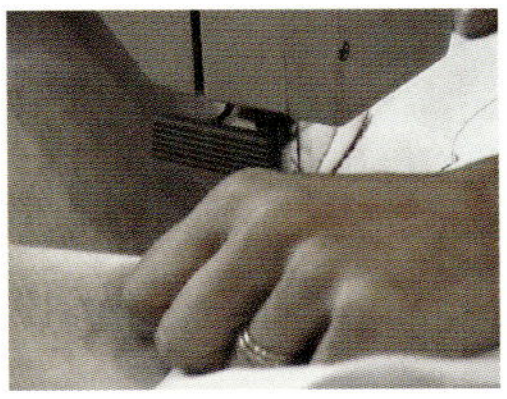
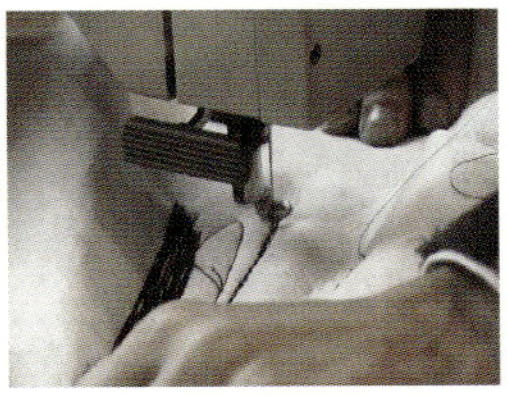
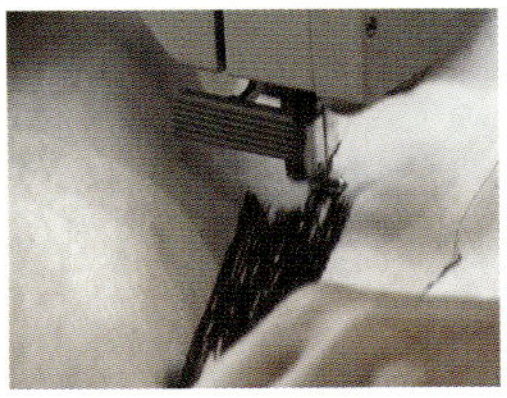
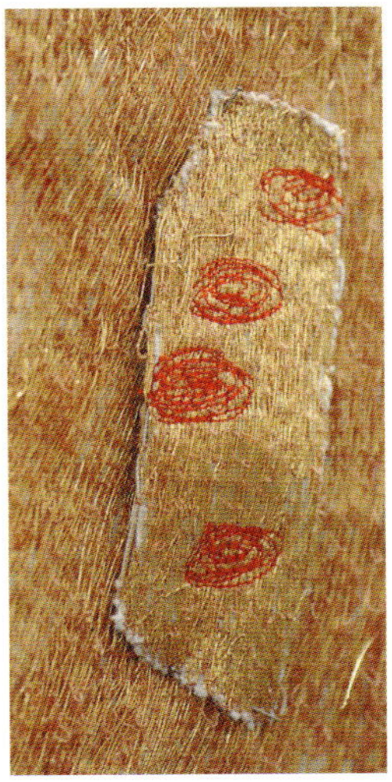

1994	Oxford Gallery, with Louise Baldwin
1994	Summer Show, Contemporary Applied Arts
1993	Visions of Craft 1972–93 Outstanding works from the Crafts Council Collection Crafts Council, London
1993	Chelsea Crafts Fair, London (also 91/89/87)
1993	Figurative Embroidered Textiles, City Gallery, Leicester
1993	Summer Show, Contemporary Applied Arts
1993	Money and Art, The Whitworth Art Gallery, Manchester
1992	Out of the Frame, Crafts Council, London, touring exhibition; (catalogue) NCCA, Sunderland; Elizabeth Gallery, Wakefield; The Mercer Gallery, Harrogate; Herbert Art Gallery and Museum, Coventry; Aberystwyth Arts Centre; Plymouth City Museum; Wakefield Art Gallery; Peter Scott Gallery, Lancaster
1992	Contemporary Textile Gallery
1992	62 Group Exhibition, Hankyu Dept Stores, Osaka, Japan
1991	Can't Stop Me Now! Crafts Council, London, (tour)
1991	Favourite Things, Crafts Council Gallery, London
1990	Stitched Textiles – a Celebration, Embroiderers' Guild Exhibition, Commonwealth Institute, London
1990	Cross Threads, Bradford Textiles Festival (tour)
1988	Tex-styles, Smiths Gallery, London
1987	Stitchery International, Pittsburgh, USA
1986	Stitched Textiles for Interiors, RIBA Gallery, London
1986	Contemporary Textile Gallery, London

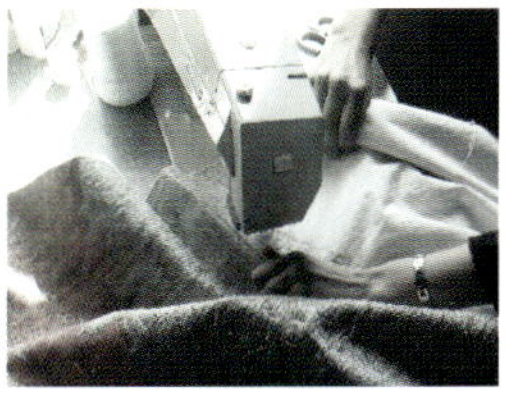

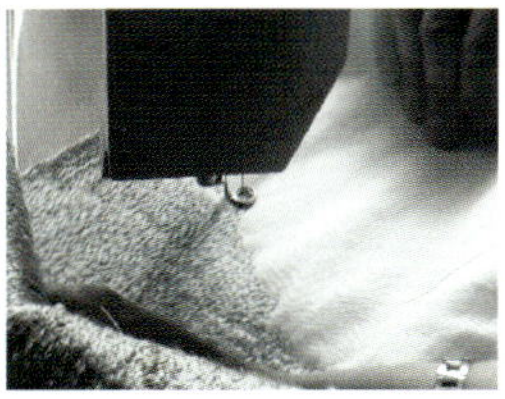

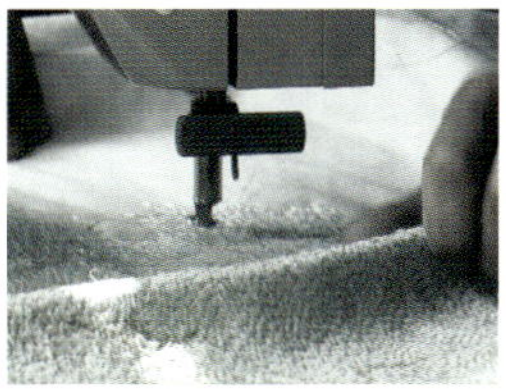

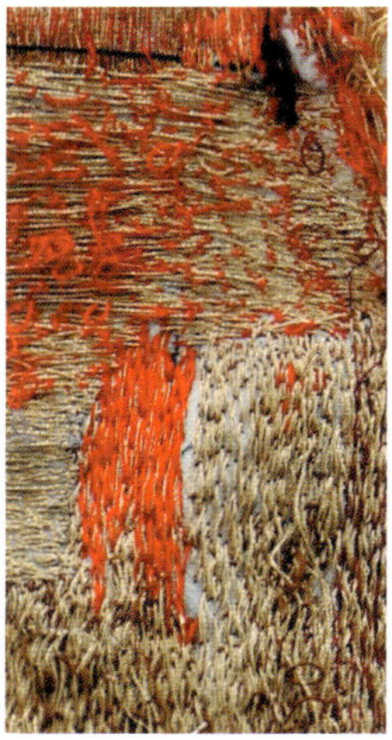

Awards

2002	Arts Council National Touring Programme award for solo touring exhibition (co-ordinated by Calderdale MBC: Museums and Arts)
2002	Mid-career Exhibition Development Award – Southern and South East Arts
1999	Kreinik Award
1999	Bernina Award
1997	Southern Arts Awards (also 92/91/88/87)
1993	Cosmopolitan achievement awards (special commendation in Creative Arts)
1991	British Council grant
1988	Taittinger Prize

1988 Crafts Council Training Scheme, Professional artist training Linda Miller
1987 Crafts Council Setting Up Grant
1985 Clothworkers' Foundation grant

Public Collections
Portsmouth City Art Gallery
The Otter Art Gallery, University College Chichester
The Whitworth Art Gallery, Manchester
Crafts Council of Great Britain
The Embroiderers' Guild
St Mary's College, Baltimore, USA
The Prudential Collection
Hampshire Museums Service
Calderdale MBC: Museums and Arts
The Embroiderers' Guild, NSW, Australia
Museo Internazionale delle Arti Applicate Oggi, Turin, Italy

Album Covers
Veil of Gossamer, Dave Bainbridge (released Autumn 2003)
Heaven's Bright Sun, Iona, 1996, Alliance Music cat no: ALD092
Eye of the Eagle, Dave Bainbridge, David Fitzgerald, David Adam, 1998, Kingsway Music cat no: KMCD2152
Yannis Constantinidis, Matthew Koumis, 1995, Etcetera Records cat no: KTC 1183

Publications
Eye of the Needle, The Textile Art of Alice Kettle, by Alice Kettle and Jennifer Harris, ed. Matthew Koumis, Telos, 1995
5000 Years of Embroidery, ed. Jennifer Harris, British Museum Publications 1993
Contemporary Embroidery, Anne Morrell, Cassell 1993
The New Textiles, Chloe Colchester, Thames & Hudson 1992
Drawing, Seeing and Observation, Ian Simpson, Redwood Press 3rd edition 1992

Periodicals
Chagall Glass at Chichester and Tudeley, Otter Memorial Paper No 14, ed. Professor Paul Foster 2002
Textile Fibre Forum Magazine, March 2001
The Textile Art of Alice Kettle, Australian Crafts, January 2001
The Embroidery Art of Alice Kettle – Expanding the definition of handwork, Ilze Aviks, FiberArts January 1997

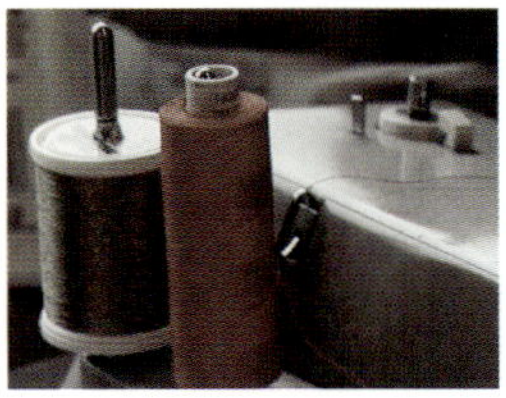
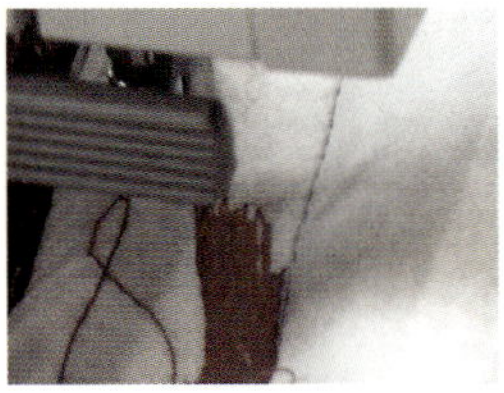
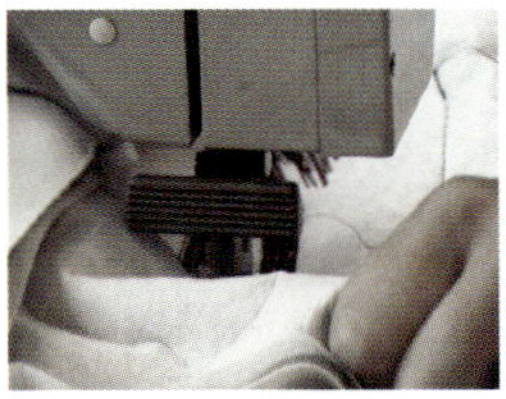
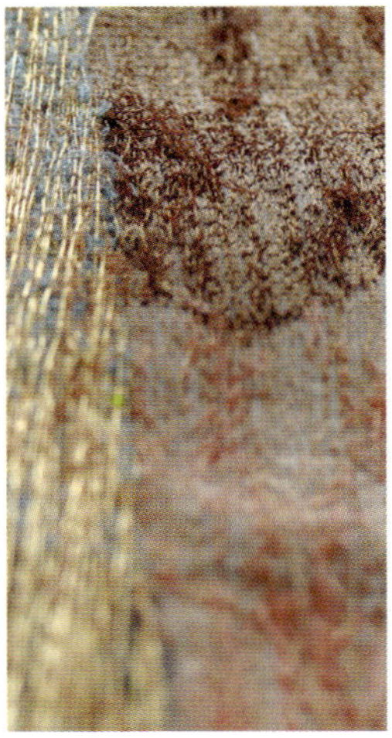

Selected Illustrated Press Articles

The Poor Relation, Ecclesiastical Embroidery, Embroidery Magazine, June 2003
Chagall Column, Embroidery Magazine, June 2003
Anne Morrell, Machine Embroidery Textiles, Volume 24 1995
Oriana, Ruth Pavey, Crafts, July 1995
Cruise Lines Leave the Doldrums, Independent on Sunday 19.3.95
Alice Makes Mark on 21st Century with World's Biggest Embroidery, Hampshire Chronicle 20.1.95
Embroidery Drawing, Country Living, April 1994
Alice in Winchester, Margot Coatts, Crafts, November 1994
P&O Push the Boat Out For Artists, Alison Roberts, The Times 10.5.94
Artist Echoes a Medieval Tradition, Hampshire Chronicle, April 1994
Swatches, Tom Lundberg, Fibre Arts, USA, Summer 1993
TextilForum, Holland, Summer 1993
International Showcase, Beautiful Home, Hong Kong, September 1992
Material Advances, Margot Coatts, Crafts, September 1992
In Context, Audrey Walker, Embroidery, Spring 1992
Spotlight on Alice Kettle, Elizabeth Benn, Embroidery, Summer 1992
Chelsea's Choice, Crafts, September 1991
Alice Kettle a Filambule, Dominique Vollichard, 24 Heurs, Lausanne, Switzerland 30.4.91
Alice Kettle, Needle Arts, USA, September 1990
Shining Kettle, Interior (International Textiles) 1988 no 3
Alice Kettle a Filambule, Emma Bernhardt, Elle Magazine, February 1988
Alice Kettle, A Formal Image, Embroidery, Autumn 1987
Embroidery at the RIBA, Anthea Godfrey, Embroidery, Winter 1986

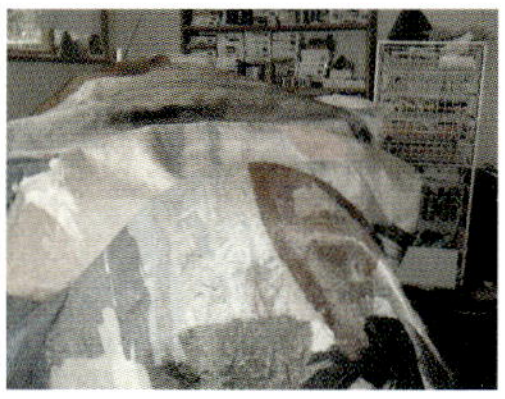

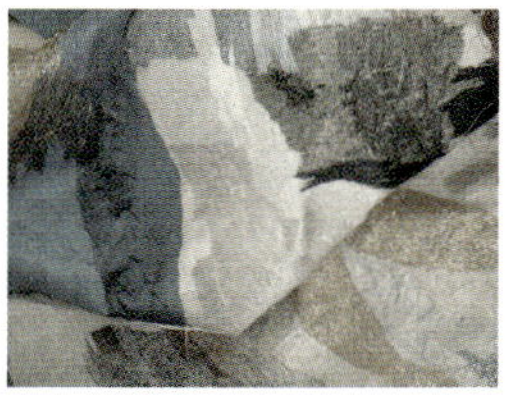

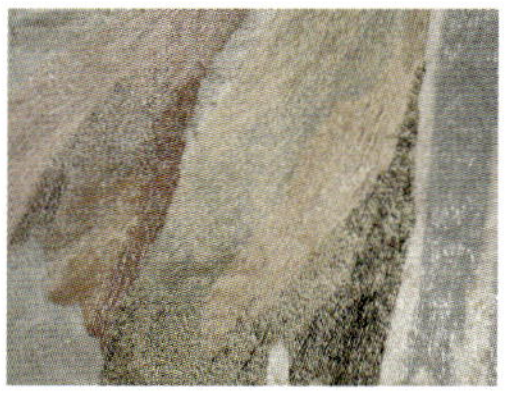

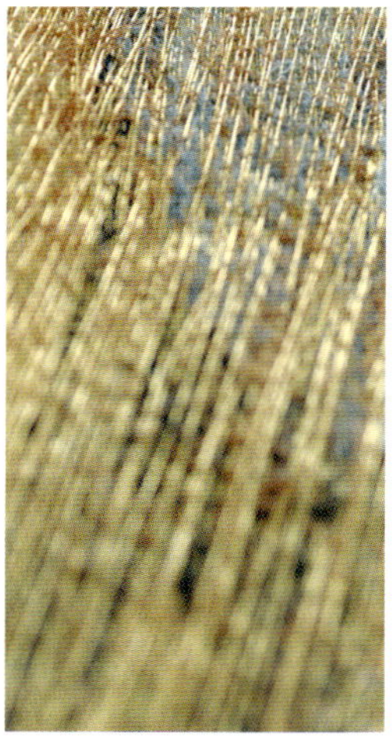

Selected Professional

2002–	Tutor, Opus School of Textiles, accredited by Middlesex University
2002–	Juror, Quilt Show, The Knitting and Stitching Show, London
1997	Artist in Residence, Canberra School of Art, Australia.
	Various lectures in colleges and universities in Australia and New Zealand
1987–91	Part time tutor, Goldsmiths' College, University of London
1987–88	Southern Arts Residency, Cowes High School, Isle of Wight

Teaching

Winchester School of Art; Royal College of Art, London; Chelsea School of Art; Goldsmiths' College; University of Ulster; Embroiderers' Guild, London; Chelsea School of Art; University College Chichester; Knuston Hall; Stitch Design, London; Quarry Bank Mill, Styal; Aspex Gallery, Portsmouth.

List of plates

page:

process: Cotton, rayon and metallic threads stitched onto canvas or felt

photography:
*James Johnson **James Newell ***Damien McDonald

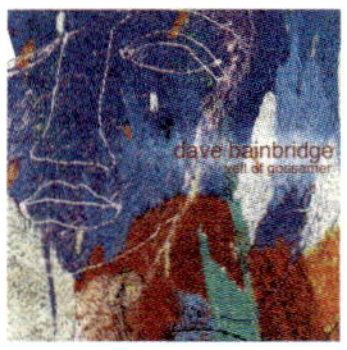

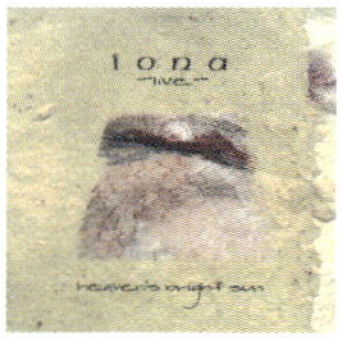

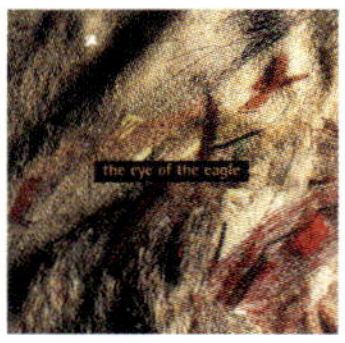

Alice Kettle's work appears on the album covers of:

Veil of Gossamer
Dave Bainbridge
(released Autumn 2003)

Heaven's Bright Sun
Iona
1996 Alliance Music
cat no: ALD092

Eye of the Eagle
Dave Bainbridge,
David Fitzgerald,
David Adam
1998 Kingsway Music
cat no: KMCD2152

Biographies

Sara Roberts works freelance in contemporary visual arts and crafts – writing, exhibition curation, and project management – and has produced publications for PACA (Public Arts Commissions Agency), The British Council, Southern Arts Touring Exhibitions Service (sates.org) and Hampshire County Council. She recently curated the exhibition *30/30 Vision, Creative Journeys in Contemporary Craft* for the Crafts Council.

Mary Schoeser is an internationally known writer and critic, and the author of several influential publications on the applied arts. Her most recent works include *More is More: an antidote to minimalism*, published by Conran Octopus (London) and Reed Publishing (NZ) Limited, and *World Textiles: a concise history*, published worldwide by Thames and Hudson in their *Story of Art* series. As a Research Fellow at Central Saint Martins College of Art & Design, she is currently curating *A Rich Seam: from peasant art to wearable art* for venues in the USA and UK.

Audrey Walker is an internationally renowned textile artist. She was head of textiles at Goldsmiths' College from 1975 to 1988, and in 1993 she was awarded the MBE for services to textiles.

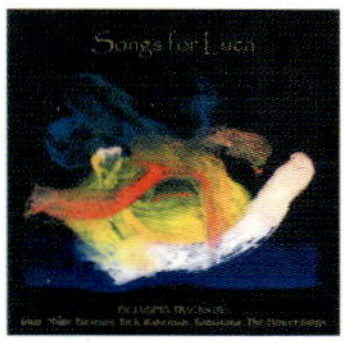

IONA's Dave Bainbridge and his wife are currently helping their autistic son Luca overcome the challenges that autism bring to his life using the Son-Rise Programme, (Autism Treatment Centre of America). A home-based, parent-led programme in a special playroom where Luca is loved and respected in a non-judgemental environment. In 'Mythscapes' Alice Kettle is producing an ongoing series of small pieces (called Luca's pictures), the proceeds of which will go to this programme.

Acknowledgements

Alice Kettle dedicates this exhibition and catalogue to Evie, and to Poppy, Tamsin and Maia, with love.

With special thanks to: Margaret Bingham, Michael Brennand-Wood, The Dean of Gloucester the Right Reverend Nicholas Bury, Lesley Butterworth, Professor Paul Foster, Dr. Enzo Biffi Gentili, John Gillett, Dr. Jennifer Harris, June Hill, Warren Horton, Philip Hughes, David Kay, Anne Leclerq, June Middleton, Keiren Phelan, Sara Roberts, Lisa Rostron, Mary Schoeser, Andrew Salmon, Diana Springall, Audrey Walker MBE, Reverend Canon Keith Walker and the extraordinary support of many friends and colleagues.

The making of *Rite of Passage* and *Towers* was assisted by Chrissie Davies and Jane Barry.

Calderdale Museums and Arts would like to thank The Arts Council of England, Beni Culturali Regione Piemonte/ MIAAO, Carcanet Press Limited, Gerald Duckworth and Co. Ltd, Dr. Enzo Biffi Gentili, Jane Gerrard, John Gillett, Jennifer Hallam, Philip Hughes, Alice Kettle, Anne Leclerq, Jim Milner, Resource: The V&A Purchase Grand Fund, Sara Roberts, Lisa Rostron, Andrew Salmon (Creative Exhibitions), Mary Schoeser, Jeremy Theophilus, Audrey Walker MBE and the Staff of Bankfield Museum.

poems

Louise Glück *Meadowlands* Carcanet Press Ltd 1998
Homer *The Odyssey* trans. EV Rieu (Penguin 1946)
Dorothy Parker *Penelope* by permission of Gerald Duckworth and Co. Ltd
Alfred, Lord Tennyson, from *The Lotos-Eaters* 1833

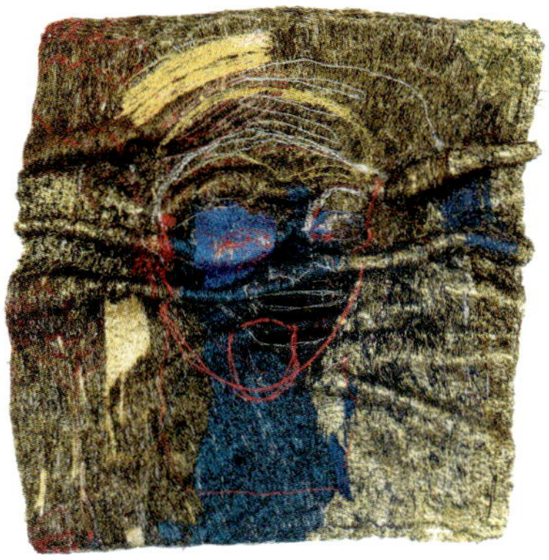

Metamorphosis

Edited by: Philip Hughes and organised by
The Gallery Ruthin Craft Centre
Designed by: lawn 01244 674531
Printed by: JT McLaughlin

Published by: Calderdale MBC Museums & Arts

ISBN 0 946115 01 X

Printed on paper sourced from
sustainable forests

Bankfield Museum, Haley Hill, Halifax
West Yorkshire HX3 6HG

CALDERDALE COUNCIL COMMUNITY SERVICES DIRECTORATE ARTS COUNCIL ENGLAND